"Through so many people's stories, ı ve come to understand that a great hardship of depression is the conviction that one suffers alone. This book contradicts that lie, not only with the author's own story but with the words of admired Christian leaders. If you live with depression, you can find hope, comfort, helpful ideas, and people like you in these pages."

Amy Simpson, author of *Troubled Minds: Mental Illness and the Church's Mission*

"Diana Gruver has written a compelling book. In it she tells the stories of seven historical figures, some but not all household names, who suffered severe depression. Gruver does it just right, avoiding the many pitfalls that could have made the book excessively sentimental or judgmental. She lets the individuals describe their own experiences, refusing to subject them to modern clinical diagnosis. She chooses quotes from their writings that are so profound, human, and powerful that I kept tearing up, drawn into the nightmare of their condition. Her writing is clear and cogent and luminous. She tells their stories with sensitivity and compassion. She gives her subjects voices, as if letting them speak across the years to us. Her commentary and reflections along the way are full of hope. This is the kind of historical writing that is both responsible and moving. I will recommend this book to my friends."

Gerald L. Sittser, professor of theology at Whitworth University and author of *A Grace Disguised*

"This book takes us into the hearts of seven people who wrestled deeply with depression and only intermittently experienced a measure of freedom and healing. Diana Gruver, who knows depression well herself, artfully and sensitively opens up their inner pain and the outer difficult circumstances of their lives, raising many big and difficult questions about the nature of intractable depression, its stigma, and why God allows some to suffer so much before taking away their tears and releasing them through death. She draws out helpful lessons from the variety of things that helped these seven men and women to keep going, even when death seemed an attractive option, and to somehow continue to believe and trust in God in the darkness. The author has researched their lives extensively, using letters and biographies to enter their worlds. Her helpful footnotes add more information and useful resources for further reading. This book is a wonderful and sensitive encouragement for any for whom life has become unbearably dark and for those who seek to help them."

Richard Winter, professor emeritus of counseling and applied theology at Covenant Theological Seminary, author of *When Life Goes Dark*

"Diana Gruver has given the church a precious gift in *Companions in the Darkness*. Every depressed Christian and his or her loved ones should read this book. Diana has labored painstakingly to unearth the previously hidden details of the stories of depressed Christians of great faith and told their stories compellingly and compassionately, chipping away at the stigma of depression in the church. The stories we tell matter, and *Companions in the Darkness* is crucial in telling the historically accurate one, revealing that the illness of depression has plagued people of great faith for centuries. It opposes using faith destructively as a judgmental hammer and instead shows how faith sustains the depressed Christian. The gospel of God's great love for his children, including those struggling with depression, cannot coexist with stigma. Thank you, Diana, for the gift of *Companions in the Darkness*."

Karen Mason, professor of counseling and psychology at Gordon-Conwell Theological Seminary

"It is rare to say that there is no other book like this, but with Diana Gruver's *Companions in the Darkness* she has done something that no other book has done: given us true companions for dark times by exploring the depression of older Christian leaders. She weaves in her own story of depression, offers contemporary psychological insight about mental health disorders, and invites us to take heart; we are not alone. Through her keen eye—an eye sensitive to suffering—she helps us understand Martin Luther's melancholy and physical pain, William Cowper's despair, Martin Luther King Jr.'s exhaustion, and Mother Teresa's dark night of the soul. These biographies are interesting and informative, but more they are manna, light, and hope. Many will be grateful for this very fine and truly helpful exploration."

Byron Borger, owner of Hearts & Minds Bookstore, Dallastown, PA

"With wise insight and palpable compassion, Diana Gruver recounts the oh-so-human stories of Christians revered across the centuries as leaders, as achievers, as exemplars. For all of their fame as 'great' Christians, these saints tasted their own radical vulnerability and knew the anguish of mental illness. To all who seek God yet suffer, there is comfort to be found in this sacred company among the brothers and sisters who lived faithfully amid struggle, the companions and guides who assure us that depression will not have the last word. Practical and deeply personal, *Companions in the Darkness* is a gift to us all."

Karen Wright Marsh, author of *Vintage Saints and Sinners* and executive director of Theological Horizons centered at the Bonhoeffer House

COMPANIONS
in the
DARKNESS

—

SEVEN SAINTS
WHO STRUGGLED
WITH DEPRESSION
AND DOUBT

—

DIANA GRUVER

FOREWORD BY
CHUCK DeGROAT

An imprint of InterVarsity Press
Downers Grove, Illinois

InterVarsity Press
P.O. Box 1400, Downers Grove, IL 60515-1426
ivpress.com
email@ivpress.com

InterVarsity Press® is the book-publishing division of InterVarsity Christian Fellowship/USA®, a movement of students and faculty active on campus at hundreds of universities, colleges, and schools of nursing in the United States of America, and a member movement of the International Fellowship of Evangelical Students. For information about local and regional activities, visit intervarsity.org.

Scripture quotations, unless otherwise noted, are from The Holy Bible, English Standard Version, copyright © 2001 by Crossway Bibles, a division of Good News Publishers. Used by permission. All rights reserved.

While any stories in this book are true, some names and identifying information may have been changed to protect the privacy of individuals.

(other permissions needed):
Cover design and image composite: David Fassett
Interior design: Daniel van Loon
Images: black & white op art © Dimitris66 / DigitalVision Vectors / Getty Images

ISBN 978-0-8308-4828-7 (print)
ISBN 978-0-8308-5338-0 (digital)

Printed in the United States of America ∞

InterVarsity Press is committed to ecological stewardship and to the conservation of natural resources in all our operations. This book was printed using sustainably sourced paper.

Library of Congress Cataloging-in-Publication Data
A catalog record for this book is available from the Library of Congress.

P 25 24 23 22 21 20 19 18 17 16 15 14 13 12 11 10 9 8 7 6 5 4 3 2 1

Y 39 38 37 36 35 34 33 32 31 30 29 28 27 26 25 24 23 22 21 20

For Lydia

May you always find light in the dark places

CONTENTS

7

MARTIN LUTHER KING JR.

Drink from the Reservoir of Resilience | *120*

CONCLUSION

The Water Is Deep, but the Bottom Is Good | *139*

ACKNOWLEDGMENTS | *143*

APPENDIX

When One You Love Is in the Dark | *145*

BRIEF BIOGRAPHIES OF THE COMPANIONS | *151*

NOTES | *163*

FOREWORD

Chuck DeGroat

You are not alone. These are the words that echoed in my being as I read Diana's *Companions in the Darkness.*

As a seminary student and young pastor in the mid-1990s, I learned about many heroes of the faith. I don't remember hearing much about melancholy, discouragement, or depression though.

It wasn't until I sunk into my own abyss that I discovered my own need for companionship. I went searching for stories, but I didn't see a work quite like this—one written by a storyteller familiar with the abyss herself and a student of the untold history of our so-called heroes.

We live in a world that bombards us with images of success, perfection, achievement, relevance, and power. Sadly, the contemporary church is often not very different. I've found myself, both as pastor and as a parishioner, walking around a church asking, "Is there anyone like me here? Anyone who knows the darkest night?"

I've also mentored and counseled pastors over the years—good, hard-working folks who believed that to be a good pastor, they'd have to keep it together at all times—who are stuffing hard emotions, hiding profound pain. Tragically, I've encountered broken marriages, moral failure, and even suicide among those trying to stay strong, to get through, to "never let them see you sweat." The cost of stuffing pain is much greater than navigating the wilderness road to freedom.

Diana is a wise guide for those of us longing for a map for the journey and a companion for those of us longing for grace on the journey. She knows the terrain, and she's studied the women and men behind the classic works of theology and spirituality we cherish so dearly.

Diana writes, "We need people who can hold us up during our struggles with depression. We need people who can shout back to us from further ahead. Depression is a fierce enemy, they say, but it need not be your victor. It need not have the last say. Your usefulness is not over. Your God has not left you. The water is deep—but the bottom is good."

Who are the "people who can hold us up"? Martin Luther and Mother Teresa, Charles Spurgeon and Martin Luther King Jr., among other saints and sages who called us to the heights but intimately knew the depths of depression. And while Diana does not pretend to be a psychologist, she offers wisdom that is psychologically sound while at the same time theologically rich and historically insightful.

Finally, Diana offers profound and compelling stories, but she does not leave us there. She calls us to meet others in the midst of their stories. She calls us to become bearers of the shared burden. She writes, "You, too, can be a guide for others through the dark, a companion in the deepest night."

I'm a better guide for reading and savoring this. You will be too.

INTRODUCTION

Defining the Darkness

I did not have a word for it until my senior year of college. Looking back, I can see it started before then, in cycles and seasons when I described myself as "down," "in a funk," "struggling," "low." My friend talked me into seeing a counselor at our college's health center, and there I was given the word: depression.

It felt foreign at first, as if this couldn't be me, couldn't be this thing I was feeling. But it had been so long since I felt emotionally steady, emotionally "up," that I didn't remember what normal felt like anymore. I no longer had the energy to wrestle with the thoughts in my head. I was stuck in a fog—confused, overwhelmed, suffocated.

For brief moments it lifted enough for me to sip the fresh air—to realize just how much clearer and easier life was without its presence. On the days it lingered, I cried myself to sleep, my body curled into a tight, self-protective ball, begging God to hear me, to make me okay.

As time went on, I wondered whether he did hear me. My tears dried up and feelings left me. When the numbness came, I lay awake, exhausted but unable to rest, desperate for those tears to return, because then I would know I was still alive, not a shell of a human being. I longed to disappear, to drift off into never-ending sleep. I longed for it all to go away.

Throughout this season, I felt weak, as if I ought to be able to fight the encroaching and all-encompassing darkness. I felt ashamed, as if I was doing something wrong. Most of all, I felt afraid, as depression tightened its grip on my sanity. Afraid of the thoughts gnawing at my mind. Afraid of how much deeper I might plunge into the pit. Afraid of my desire to cease to exist.

I survived. With the help of therapy, medication, a good support system, and God's grace, the light slowly dawned. Life gradually became easier, the days less daunting. My mind could focus and process once again. I could turn loving attention on other people. Sleep was no longer elusive. The sensation of joy once again took up residence in my heart.

I felt like one of the lucky ones—like I had barely survived my brush with depression's darkness. I was thankful to be alive, returned once again to the sun. But I didn't know what to do with my experience. I didn't know what to do with the marks it left on me. I didn't know what I would do if it returned.

And return it did, this time while I was living abroad, working as an administrator and a housemom in a home full of foster children. Once again came the darkness, the tears, the exhaustion. Stripped of my usual support network, I once again needed medication to help me as I clawed toward the light.

Months later, stable but still on this latest round of antidepressants, I found myself in a seminary classroom scribbling names from church history in the margins of my notebooks. With the battle of depression still fresh in my mind, I recognized something in my professor's asides about different historical figures. These brothers and sisters were like friends whispering to me from centuries past. They, too, had been plunged into darkness. They, too, had been depressed.

So I set out on a journey to get to know them and others like them and to learn the lessons they might offer from the darkness.

WHAT IS DEPRESSION?

Those of us who suffer from depression call it many things. The fog. The black dog. The darkness. The unholy ghost. We dance around it with metaphors and paint pictures of the pain with our words. The word *depression* is too clinical, the list of symptoms too sterile.

Diagnostic guidelines cannot describe the sensation that your heart has stopped beating, has been torn from your chest, while your body continues to move mechanically, numb, without its lifeblood. I am a puppet. I am a ghost. I float invisible, unfeeling, watching the alive ones laugh and love. No mere definition can explain that feeling of emptiness, of isolation, of vacant pain.

Some people think depression is sadness. But it is deeper than that. The feeling of clearly defined and attributable sadness would be a relief. Instead I am overcome with too much feeling, awash with a vague, gnawing sorrow. I weep and writhe under its weight, and then in a more terrifying turn, I feel so much that I feel nothing at all. I am still and numb. I would welcome sadness, for then I would know I am still alive. As it is, I am the walking dead.

Medical professionals, however, don't work in word pictures. They distill depression into a list of symptoms, as stated in the official diagnostic manual, the *DSM-5*:

- depressed mood
- loss of interest or pleasure in things or activities you once enjoyed
- increased or decreased appetite or unexplained weight loss or gain
- fatigue or loss of energy
- sleep difficulties—either insomnia or sleeping more than usual
- noticeable slowing down of thoughts and physical movement or noticeable agitation and restlessness
- difficulty concentrating and making decisions

- feelings of worthlessness or excessive guilt
- thoughts or plans of suicide or recurring thoughts of death[1]

To be diagnosed with depression, a person must have at least five of these symptoms for a two-week period, and at least one of them must be either a depressed mood or the loss of interest and pleasure in activities they once enjoyed. Symptoms must also cause distress and interfere with a person's ability to function in work or social settings.

Though the anguish depression causes may make this way of defining it feel cold, specific definitions do, at least, remind us that depression is a real illness. It has symptoms and diagnostic criteria, and it requires the intervention of medical and mental health professionals. It may require medication and therapy. It can be deadly. It is not "just in your head." It is not something we can defeat by forcing "mind over matter." It's something to be taken seriously.

THE MANY FACES OF DEPRESSION

Reading through symptoms like a checklist blurs the reality that depression wears many faces.

It is the student who cuts class to lay uncaring in a dark room, her mind too muddled to listen to a lecture, her heart too overwhelmed to produce speech for one more human being.

It is the bereaved father whose grief erodes his ability to think, to live, to rest, to heal. Whose body aches with the act of breathing. Who cannot summon energy to return to work—or even to rise from bed. The father whose grief is leading him nowhere but deeper into an irreparable pit of despair.

It is the young professional who continues to push through apathy and sleepless nights. The one who goes through the motions of dress, of food, of meetings, of sitting in the chair, but whose life is drained of all vigor.

It is the man devoid of hope who is standing on a bridge, a note at home for his wife, every cell aching for an end to the pain.

Depression morphs and shifts around the criteria we use to diagnose it. It can come from an accumulation of painful circumstances. It can come without warning. Some of us continue to get out of bed and attend school or work. Others lay immobile in the dark. Physical symptoms overwhelm some of us more than others, especially in cultures particularly laden with stigma. It differs in severity and in the length of time it takes up its chilling residence in our bones.

The people you will meet in these pages reflect this complex variation. Some continued haltingly with their work while others were incapacitated. Some experienced other physical illnesses or symptoms along with their psychological ones. Some seemed to have a family proclivity to depression, suggesting a genetic component. For some, depression was sparked by trauma, loneliness, and difficulty. Others found that it took hold with little warning.

It is not my desire to diagnose each of these people with what we now call clinical depression. It would be historically irresponsible and foolish to attempt to do so from afar, across the distance of culture and time. However, I find in each of these women and men a set of symptoms, a collection of metaphors, a description of mind and heart remarkably akin to the experience we now call depression. I don't need a diagnosis to find fellowship in their stories or receive their wisdom.

DEPRESSION: A BRIEF HISTORY

The plight of depression is not only a modern one. Over the centuries we've merely blamed it on different causes, targeted it with different cures, and referred to it by different names. The people whose stories you will read in these pages, for example, may not have called their struggle "depression," as I do. For some it was "melancholy" or "a disorder of humors." Others didn't give a name to it at all. But all the while its basic description has remained the same.

The understanding of depression in the West has shifted with culture and with our approach to disease as a whole. Throughout this development, I see cycling patterns of thought: Is depression an illness, a source of inspiration, or a personal fault? Always caught in the midst of the debates and shifting theories, of course, are the people themselves who suffer. Their illness (or curse or source of genius depending on the opinion at hand) is debated by doctors and philosophers while they struggle for the desire to live.

The physicians of the ancient Greco-Roman world saw depression as a disease of the body. At that time, and for many centuries after, the body was believed to react to a balance of four essential liquids, the four humors. Depression was attributed to an excess of one of them, black bile. (This humoral theory continued to influence the understanding and treatment of depression through at least the seventeenth century.) A person could have a natural proclivity toward this imbalance, but it could also be triggered by external, environmental factors.

Physicians like Hippocrates, Rufus of Ephesus, and Galen developed treatments that targeted the physical cause and included diet and oral remedies to adjust the levels of black bile. They also encouraged treatments that targeted environmental factors and counteracted the patient's sorrow, such as travel, massage, exercise, and diverting activities.[2] This ancient approach to depression is similar to what we understand to be effective today, combining the treatment of a body out of balance (though now we talk about chemicals in the brain and not black bile) with lifestyle adjustments. Unfortunately, this was not always the case in the millennia to follow.

While Greco-Roman physicians proposed cures, the Greek philosopher Aristotle portrayed depression in a slightly less negative light. Melancholy was not only a disease, he argued. It could be the seat of inspiration. The melancholy temperament, or the temperament that gave people an innate propensity to depression, also inclined people to greatness, creativity, and genius. People of such a temperament were at greater risk for insanity, but they were also poised to excel in fields such as philosophy, poetry, and art.[3]

Aristotle's idea of the melancholy genius would resurface centuries later in the Renaissance and again in the Romantic period. During these times, melancholy was once again believed to be a necessary part of brilliance, creativity, and deep insight into the world. Depression became esteemed and stylish enough to be imitated. Aristocrats and aspiring geniuses mimicked the languor of those who genuinely suffered and discovered they rather liked the practice.[4] I can only imagine being a severely depressed person watching others enjoy what they perceived to be your state, without realizing the interior desperation that accompanied it.

Of course, there were also periods when depression was not held in such high esteem. Instead of being seen as an illness of the body, it was seen as an illness of the soul. As such, it was considered a sin or the influence of demons. In some cases, this view sprang from biblically inspired logic. Augustine, for example, argued that reason was what separated humankind from beasts, so the loss of reason in melancholy must indeed be a sign of God's punishment.[5] And some church leaders pointed to the suicide of Judas (Matthew 27) and the insanity of Nebuchadnezzar (Daniel 4) as evidence that mental illness was a sign of sin and God's judgment.[6]

One of the "deadly sins," or cardinal vices, identified by the desert fathers and mothers and early monastic communities looked similar to depression. In its original forms, acedia, which we now call sloth, was more than just the apathy and laziness we've come to associate with it today. It was connected early on to another "sin," tristitia, which brought with it the connotation of sorrow and sadness. As the definition of acedia developed, it took on a form akin to depression, marked by exhaustion, sadness, restlessness, apathy, sluggishness, despair, and neglect.[7] We cannot simply equate acedia with what we now call depression, but they bear strong enough similarities that it's possible some early monks who were chastised because of the sin of acedia were actually suffering from depression.

The condemnation continued. In the Inquisition, some faced fines and imprisonment for their "sin" of depression.[8] Much later, depression was blamed on a decadent, self-indulgent, and morally decaying society—and people's participation in its degradation.[9]

Though the terminology may not be the same, many today still view depression as a sin and question a depressed person's salvation, hint at a lack of spiritual maturity, or probe into what abiding sin could have caused such despondency. Much like Christians in ages past, they chastise the depressed person or simply withdraw from them so as not to be contaminated themselves. Though depressed people might not be thrown in prison, many of them still experience ostracism, shame, and blame in the church. Not much has changed.

Definitions by the church were not the only sources of abuse for the depressed. The eighteenth century bears the shame of the heyday of asylums of horrors, like the infamous Bedlam in London.[10] Pity the person given up as insane by their relatives and locked away like an animal for the rest of their days in such an institution. And pity the person who was more mildly depressed but was desperate to maintain enough sanity to avoid such a place. In addition to the physical torture offered as "treatment," the hospital allowed visitors to come observe its mentally ill patients for a fee, making a public spectacle of its residents. Fortunately, the conditions of such asylums improved over time as the result of major legal and social reforms regarding the care of the mentally ill.

In the midst of the cycling approaches to depression since the days of Hippocrates, scientific understandings of the human body have developed, furthering our understanding of depression. No longer do we attribute our disorders of body and mind to misbalanced humors. Now, we approach depression in terms of brain chemistry and psychology. When these two pieces are pitted against each other (as some have done), the tension over what to blame for depression continues. Is it a breakdown of the body or of the mind (or soul)? Is it caused by genes or by circumstance? Is it solved through antidepressants or digging into thought patterns? When we hold brain chemistry and psychology together, though, we grow closer to finding a middle road, one that treats depression in terms of the whole person, with medication and therapy working in concert and with a support system and faith and lifestyle as important contributing factors of wellness.

In some ways, we've come far in our understanding of mental illness. In other ways, we're still shaking off the problematic attitudes of our forebears. In still other ways, we've merely returned to what the ancients told us millennia ago.

BUT . . . THEY DIDN'T TAKE ANTIDEPRESSANTS

Since the days of bloodletting and mental asylums, our interventions for depression have advanced significantly. Though we still have a lot to learn about the complex inner workings of the brain, we do have access to treatments for depression that can result in relief for most people. A combination of medication and therapy is extremely effective in treating depression, and some lifestyle changes (like exercise, for example) can be helpful in addition to these treatments.

This is where I must plead with you. If you or someone you love is struggling with depression—if the symptoms here and the stories in this book sound familiar—please seek the help of a professional. I am not a doctor or a therapist. Neither is anyone featured in this book. We cannot offer you the sufficient help you need to be well. All we can offer is the stories of our survival as fellow sufferers and brothers and sisters in Christ. We can offer advice as friends today can, sharing life experience, the lessons we've learned, the ways we've coped from day to day. This wisdom, these stories of survival, are an important part of the journey toward wellness, but they do not replace the role of any professional care you are—or need to be—receiving.

Most of the people in this book did not have access to the tools and resources we have in modern mental health care. They lived in cultures and times that did not understand the effects of depression on the brain, did not have practitioners of evidence-based therapies, and did not have the option of psychotropic medication. So their experiences and advice laid out in the coming pages do not involve pills or therapy. That does not mean that these are not helpful, recommended, and sometimes necessary to recover from depression, or that you should not seek them out if you need them. In other words, the lack of their presence does not mean they aren't important—especially considering it wasn't even an option. I often wonder how their lives and legacies might differ if they'd had access to these tools.

So please take these words and these stories and treasure them in your heart. Let them inspire and encourage you. But don't let them keep you from the care you need.

THE ROLE OF FAITH

At this point, many will start to ask, "But I'm a Christian. Doesn't my faith play a role when I'm depressed?"

Yes. I believe the life of faith plays a critical role. But it plays a role similar to what it plays with other illnesses.

When a family member is diagnosed with cancer, we pray for healing. We find comfort in the truths of the Bible. We cling to the hope of the gospel—a hope beyond our circumstances. We are open to God graciously empowering us to grow through the trial. We are surrounded by the support of our faith community, propped up by our spiritual family. But we also seek good medical care. We take medication faithfully. We keep our doctor's appointments and adhere to his or her advice.

So it is with mental illness. My faith can uphold and encourage me in the midst of the trial of depression, but it does not negate the importance of good medical care. And yes, I pray for God's healing, but I also go to the doctor and take my medication faithfully. I tape

Bible verses to my wall to see each day, but I also keep my therapy appointments. I read my Bible, but I also exercise and eat healthy and try to get rest and surround myself with as much delight as I can muster.

I personally doubt I would have survived my struggles with depression without my faith in Jesus. But it didn't stop me from seeing a doctor.

WHY WE NEED THESE STORIES

As I slogged through seasons of depression—and as I've looked back on those seasons from more stable footing—I have found the stories and presence of others who have experienced depression to be invaluable. I hear a hint of something I recognize—an aside, a metaphor, a clue that points to those marks left by the darkness—and I zero in on them. *There is someone who knows*, I think, *someone who understands. They, too, have walked through the valley of the shadow of depression.* There's something about it that binds us, like brothers in arms—the battle we have fought knits us together.

Their stories bring me comfort, reassuring me that I am not alone. They remind me I am not the only one to walk this road, that this experience is not an alien one. The lie that "surely no one has felt this" is cut down by the truth that others, in fact, have, and their presence makes me feel less isolated. These fellow travelers are my companions in the darkness of night.

They offer me wisdom—advice hard-bought on how to survive. On the lessons they learned. Of the tools they gained.

They give me hope—hope that this is not the end of my story, that I, too, will survive this. Hope that depression will not have the last say. I hear their stories of survival and perseverance, and I have hope to keep going, keep fighting, keep doing the hard work of getting well.

This is true of those I find alive today. For those I can talk to and sit down for coffee with, for those I call or write. It is the case for the leaders I encounter, those who are vulnerable enough to share their struggles. It's the case for the artists who write songs and poems, who paint or create films rooted in their experience. It is also true of those who no longer walk this earth, those who, through their letters, journals, and written accounts, leave us the legacy of their stories.

But the stories in this book were not chosen at random. They come from some of our heroes, from those whose tales we still tell long after their death. This gives them something unique to offer.

These stories from our heroes help break the guilt and stigma surrounding depression in the church—undermining the lies that I am failing, that I am a "bad Christian," that I should be better than this, or that if only I were more faithful or holy or strong this would not be happening to me. Can you imagine the audacity of applying this principle to the brothers and sisters in this book? Of telling Charles Spurgeon to read his Bible more? Or David Brainerd to pray more? Or Mother Teresa to just choose joy? We regard these people as giants of the faith, as "saints," and yet they still struggled with depression. The faithfulness of their lives did not make them immune—and it will not make me immune. They remind us that sometimes these things happen. Sometimes we are weighed down by sadness. Sometimes our brains get sick just as our bodies do. Their lives bear witness to this truth.

• • •

Since that seminary classroom where I first encountered these companions, I've come to realize that the stories we choose to tell communicate something. Ignoring a struggle like depression in the lives of people in church history—those we still talk about today, those we may call heroes—communicates something. It says those stories don't matter, or, worse, that we should be ashamed of them.

That is why this book exists. The stories you will read in this book need to be told. They need to be told so that we can be heirs of the wisdom and comfort these brothers and sisters have to share. They need to be told so that we find the courage and freedom to tell our own stories. They need to be told so that we are reminded that God can still use us, that depression will not be our life's epitaph. They are, for me, models of what it looks like to follow Jesus through depression.

If you don't struggle with depression, I hope that in these pages you find testimonies of what this struggle is like for so many people around you. I hope your humble "listening in" to these stories increases your compassion and your awareness of how to help your depressed brothers and sisters.

If you, like me, are no stranger to depression, I hope that as you read, you find a "friend" along the way. Someone whose experience you recognize and can find camaraderie with. Someone who can whisper, "Yes, I've been there. I know." Someone who can offer a little advice about how to survive, how to be faithful. May they bring you comfort. May they bring you hope. May they shine a little light on your path through the dark.

1

MARTIN LUTHER

Flee Solitude—Drink, Joke, and Jest

An ebony stain followed in the wake of his jerking arm movements across the page. Words poured from him. Dark ink flung at dark thoughts, keeping them at bay, feeding faith's flame.

What if your doctrine is false and in error? What if all this havoc is for naught? All you have unearthed is violence and contention.

The thoughts circled him like a hungry dog cornering its prey, eager to sink its teeth fatally through soft flesh. He met them with more ferocious scribbling with his pen.

The torment continued. He could feel the sweat beading on his face. He could smell its sour scent. It threatened to drip on the page of his letter to his friend Philip as he wrote, "I do not wish you to worry about me at all. As regards my person, everything is well, except that my mental trouble has not ceased and my former infirmity of spirit and of faith continues."[1]

The old plague had returned. The doubts, the questions, the fear. He heard the words of his old mentor in his mind. *Look to the wounds of Christ, Martin. Look at the blood pouring from his broken body.*

His voice echoed in the small, wood-paneled room. "Devil, my cause is grounded in the Gospel, the Gospel God has given me. Talk to him about it. He has commanded me to listen to Christ."[2]

It was in the name of Christ he had started. Christ would not abandon him.

But here he was, locked away in this exile, this wilderness, nestled up on this hill with the birds.

I am here with nothing to do, like a free man among captives.[3]

He glanced at the Greek New Testament on his writing table. He had nothing to do but write. Nothing to do but wrestle with Greek verbs. He would translate the New Testament. He would fill the emptiness of his tiny rooms with the Word of God. He would give the Word to the people in a language they could understand.

He pressed a hand to his stomach as nausea rose inside. His abdomen was hard and unyielding. The attacks came not only to his mind but to his body as well. Would neither of them subside?

"I did not sleep all night, and still have no peace. Please pray for me, for this malady will become unbearable, if it goes on as it has begun."[4]

"I am growing sluggish and languid and cold in spirit, and am miserable. Until to-day I have been constipated for six days."[5]

Perhaps he would die here. Alone. In agony.

They'd brought him here for safety, and he had willingly played the part, growing out the tonsure on the top of his head and adding a beard. He'd taken on the persona of a knight—Knight George— though a strange knight surely, for he spent so much time sequestered in his rooms, writing and studying.

As he gazed down at the town below, secluded, reclusive, he wondered when this exile would end. Safety had become a prison.

"I would rather burn in live coals than rot here alone, half-alive and yet not dead."[6]

CHRIST THE HANGMAN: DARK DAYS IN THE MONASTERY

By the time Martin Luther found himself sequestered in Wartburg Castle, he had sparked the religious movement we've now come to know as the Protestant Reformation. But in the years before the Reformation, before the councils and debates and disputations, Martin Luther was a monk.

It all started on a summer day as Luther was riding home from the University of Erfurt, where he was studying for a career in law. A thunderstorm caught him out in the open, terrifying him with explosions of thunder and lightning. He cowered on the ground, certain of death, and made a vow that would change his life: "St. Anne, save me, and I will become a monk!" He survived the storm and kept his vow. Within weeks he quit school, sold his books, and entered an Augustinian monastery. His father was furious at this "waste" of his education.

Once in the monastery, he threw himself into the religious life. He would later say, "I was a good monk, and I kept the rule of my order so strictly that I may say that if ever a monk got to heaven by his monkery it was I."[7] But he wasn't living the life of a peaceful contemplative. Rather, he went through his days under the shadow of desperation and fear, obsessed with living a holy life, petrified of God's judgment. He constantly doubted God's love and despaired of any hope of salvation. As he nitpicked his sins and heaped extreme forms of penance on himself, Luther was convinced his soul was damned: "I lost touch with Christ the Savior and Comforter, and made him the jailer and hangman of my poor soul."[8]

The first time Luther presided over the Mass, he feared God would strike him dead on the spot. Feeling his anxious frame trembling, he clung to the altar for support. Legend has it his hands shook so badly that he nearly spilled the Eucharistic wine.

In the midst of this turmoil, Luther's beloved confessor, mentor, and friend, Johann von Staupitz, gave him a Bible and pointed his eyes away from his own unworthiness to Jesus on the cross. In response to Luther's crippling fears, to his guilt and feelings of never measuring up, to the penance and punishment he derived for himself, to his visions of Christ only as a judge ready to smite him, Staupitz had a clear, resounding refrain: "Look to the wounds of Christ."

As Luther studied the Bible, first as a doctoral student and then as a professor in Wittenberg, and as he continued to follow Staupitz's advice, his picture of God began to shift. Instead of an angry, judgment-hungry God, peering down from heaven, ready for any excuse to strike him dead, Luther saw God as Father, freely offering forgiveness through faith by grace. Working through his despair led him to a new understanding of the gospel—the God who is for us, seen in Jesus Christ on the cross, who took on our pain and our sin to make us his children. This reclaimed gospel message was at the heart of the Protestant Reformation.

Luther called the inner turmoil and depressive angst he experienced *anfechtung*. Throughout his life, he continued to use this word to describe the terror, despair, and fear of religious crises and trials. These moments were battles for faith for him—battles to hold fast to the truth that God had not forsaken him, that he was no longer under condemnation because of Christ. They were battles to hold fast to the Word of God.

Luther's term *anfechtung* is much broader than what we call depression today, so they aren't fully synonymous terms, but they are related. They both bring the same swirling thoughts, the same internal terror. They both plague us with questions of our worthiness, of our guilt, of whether we are deserving of love. Both can make us doubt God's goodness and wonder if we can slip beyond his grace.

So in the midst of depression, when we fall under the harassment of guilt and shame, we can follow Staupitz's advice as well. *Look to the wounds of Christ.* For this is where we see the extent of God's love, the upside-down way he brings beauty and wholeness, the full measure of his grace. It is where we are reminded of truth outside of our feelings—that nothing can separate us from God's love, not even the deepest depression. Luther's life tells us this: the wounds of Christ will guide us through the darkness.

As I look back now, I realize that my seasons of depression solidified my understanding of the gospel more than any other experience in my life. God met me in the place where I felt furthest from him, and he wove strength into a message I'd heard since I was a child. I was desperate, helpless, and broken. I needed something bigger than my pain, something strong enough to bear the suffocating weight of it. I needed hope that my pain was not the end of the story. In that darkness, I was showered with a message of grace, which told the tale of One who came to me in my brokenness and offered redemption. The gospel gave me space to be "not okay" because it expected I would come needy. It offered a message of a Savior who not only offered salvation for my soul but who promised to radically remake and transform all of creation, eradicating sorrow and sickness—even faulty brain chemistry. This hope was something I could look to as truth, even as I struggled to know which of my own thoughts could be trusted. In the midst of my darkness, it became my only place of sure footing.

This does not mean that focusing on the gospel will cure our depression. It didn't for Luther, even as his theology shifted with the Reformation. Anxiety and depression would continue to afflict him for the rest of his life, and he would return to the message of the cross again and again as an antidote for his feelings of hopelessness and guilt. But his depression did become a training ground for him. He would say later that he didn't learn his theology all at once, and that his "spiritual trials" (*anfechtung*) helped him in the process.[9] He started as a depressed monk, poring over Scripture in his desperation, but as he "looked to the wounds of Christ," a light of hope slowly dawned. The spiritual darkness of one man gave birth to a new understanding of the gospel, one that transformed him and would shake the foundations of Western Christianity.

REFORMATION BEGINNINGS AND ANGUISH AT WARTBURG

Luther's shifting theology soon became a matter of public debate after he issued his Ninety-Five Theses. (It's worth noting that there is some scholarly debate about how fully formed Luther's reformation theology was at that point.) The Ninety-Five Theses were the academic result of Luther's pastoral concern over the selling of indulgences, a practice he saw devolving into a scam that abused the laypeople. His words spread quickly and widely because of the newly developed Gutenberg printing press, and the results were far more explosive than he likely intended. He'd wanted a scholarly debate. Instead he received public scrutiny and church discipline. He'd wanted reform. Instead he was facing a complete break from the church he loved and had surrendered his life to.

What followed was a rapid series of councils—with his monastic order, with church officials, with German officials—and lots of written arguments from all sides about his views. When Luther refused to recant or withdraw his previous writings, the pope excommunicated him from the church.

It all culminated in the Diet of Worms, where Luther was brought before political leaders and put on trial for heresy. His life was at risk. He would not have been the first rebel burned at the stake for his revolutionary views. Luther bravely held his ground, refusing to recant unless someone could prove from Scripture that he was wrong. The Edict of Worms that followed made him an outlaw and his writings illegal. It was a crime to offer Luther food and shelter, and he was to be captured, even if he was killed in the process.

It was on the way home from this Diet of Worms, under the shadow of this Edict, that Luther was kidnapped by friends, with the help of a supportive local political figure, Elector Frederick the Wise, and hidden in Wartburg Castle. No one knew of his whereabouts. Some assumed he was dead.

There he sat for ten months. Excommunicated from the church. A fugitive. Under threat of death. With an exploding religious movement under his care. All within four years of his first call for debate over the Ninety-Five Theses. All before his fortieth birthday.

It's enough to make my head spin.

It's no wonder Luther speaks of emotional, mental, and spiritual trials while he's in Wartburg Castle. He was stricken by health problems that brought physical agony. He was isolated and lonely, cut off from his closest friends during a volatile season, begging them to write, wary of revealing his location. He once again battled the *anfechtung* of the monastery, once again fought his "infirmity of spirit and of faith."

In spite of these struggles, Luther's productivity was superhuman. During his time in Wartburg, he wrote several pamphlets explaining and defending the Reformation, and he translated the entire New Testament into German in a matter of weeks.

Some point to this unbelievable productivity and claim there's no way Luther could have been depressed. Others point to it as evidence that he was "throwing ink at the Devil"[10] as a means to keep his dark and morbid thoughts at bay. When I read Luther's own words, I can't help but believe it's the latter.[11]

THE DEVIL LIES IN WAIT FOR YOU

Luther's understanding of the devil's role in the world is worth noting here. It's particularly important in light of how depression has been overspiritualized and treated poorly at times.

In Luther's view, the world was awash with spiritual forces at work behind the scenes, and the devil was constantly wreaking havoc. It should come as no surprise, then, that he understood the source of his (and others') depressions to be the devil himself.[12] This did not put mental illness in a special category though, as he understood the devil to be responsible for all illnesses and mishaps—even a stubbed toe. Depression and other mental illnesses were no different. Luther said of suicide, "'Tis the devil who has put the cord round their necks, or the knife to their throats."[13] He considered solitude particularly dangerous for people struggling with depression because it gives more space for the devil to "wriggle in" with his arsenal of dark thoughts, hopelessness, temptation, and lies. Scripture tells us that our enemy, the devil, seeks to "steal and kill and destroy" (John 10:10), and in this sense, even coming from a modern, Western worldview, we can recognize his delight in seeing us robbed of pleasure, dead in spirit, and possibly destroying our bodies.

So when you read about Luther attributing depression to the devil or including fighting the devil as part of his suggested cure, view his words in light of his worldview as a whole. He fought the devil when he was melancholy because in his understanding that was getting to the source. And, again, he was just as quick to talk about fighting the devil in the midst of his other health ailments. He knew all of these trials could distract from the freedom and comfort of the gospel, so he fought back. I'll let you do your own reading on all Luther has to say about combating the devil (be prepared for some lively commentary). In short, he armed himself with Scripture, sang music, and mocked the devil, focusing on the devil's impotence in the face of Christ's victory. And he looked to the hope and comfort of Christ, our victor, our gracious Lord.

Luther learned this battle in his monastery days as he battled his *anfechtungen*, and he engaged in it again in Wartburg as he furiously wrote and translated. It's the tactic he took every time the clutches of despair grasped at his mind.

STRENGTH SOON DEJECTED: LUTHER'S ILLNESSES

After ten months of exile, Luther left Wartburg Castle and returned to Wittenberg to give leadership to the growing Reformation movement. It was a dangerous decision, as nothing had changed legally since he went into hiding, but the extreme and violent interpretations of his views that were emerging demanded urgent attention. Once settled again in Wittenberg, Luther set to work organizing the Protestant churches. He wrote a simpler liturgy in German for use in worship and a *Large Catechism* and *Small Catechism* for teaching and prayer. He also clarified the role of the sacraments and reduced them from seven to two: baptism and the Lord's Supper.

In addition, much to the surprise of his friends, Luther married suddenly at the age of forty-one. His wife, Katharina von Bora, had escaped from a convent a few years earlier by hiding in old fish barrels. From what we know of Katie Luther, she was feisty, a firestorm of productivity, and possessed a stubborn streak to match her husband's. Katie and Martin Luther would have six children together. By all accounts, they came to deeply love each other and shared a happy marriage.

For a wedding present, they were given the Black Cloister in Wittenberg. It was the same Augustinian monastery Luther had lived in before the Reformation began. The halls that once whispered with the prayers and studies of monks became their home, now echoing with the lively conversations of Luther and his students, the prattle of children, and the comings and goings of the growing Reformation.

Throughout this bustling activity of life and ministry, Luther was often a sick man. In addition to extreme constipation, like he had suffered at Wartburg Castle, he developed kidney and bladder stones. The pain from them was so excruciating that he would compare them to death. He experienced a persistent ringing in his ears, vertigo, dizziness, fainting spells, and headaches, which some have suggested was Ménière's disease. He would also develop arthritis, as well as the heart problems that would eventually lead to his death.

After this long list of Luther's physical ailments, I must pause for a brief aside. Luther has received criticism for his extreme and vulgar written attacks against his theological and political opponents. Toward the end of his life, he spoke out extensively against the Jews in what can only be described as despicably anti-Semitic rhetoric. There is no end to the examples of his sharp and irritable tongue. Though it by no means comes close to excusing his behavior, I wonder if the physical and emotional struggle going on behind the scenes served to amplify this part of Luther's personality. Many of us, after all, could tell stories of the emotional toll taken by lingering and unresolved medical problems and the ways that physical and psychological struggles become intertwined.[14] Surely speaking from his own experience, Luther said, "Heavy thoughts bring on physical maladies; when the soul is oppressed, so is the body. . . . When cares, heavy cogitations, sorrows, and passions superabound, they weaken the body."[15] The reverse is also true.

We have a good example of this connection of body and spirit in an intense health scare Luther had when he was forty-three years old. His friend Justus Jonas left us a firsthand account of it.[16]

Luther had not been well. He excused himself from dinner because of a loud roaring in his ear, but as he reached his bed, he collapsed, though he remained conscious. It's clear he thought he was dying. He prayed again and again, always concluding, "Thy will be done." He told God the things he wished he'd been able to do with more time. He said goodbye to Katie and to their son, Hans, entrusting them to God's keeping, asking them to accept God's will if he should die. He was sobbing. They were sobbing. It's heartrending.

Of course, Luther didn't die then, although he would continue to complain of similar symptoms for the rest of his life. But there was more going on that day than a physical near-death experience. That morning, before his attack, Luther told his friends that he wrestled with a "grave spiritual trial." Jonas wrote the day after, "To-day the doctor [Luther] said to me: 'I must make a note of this day; yesterday I was at school.' He said that his spiritual trial of yesterday was twice as great as this bodily illness which came on in the evening."[17]

Though he spoke of this trial to his friends, we unfortunately aren't given many details. We do know that it troubled and distressed him greatly. About a month later, he wrote to his friend Philip Melanchthon, presumably about the same episode(s):

> I was for more than a whole week in death and hell, so that I was sick all over, and my limbs still tremble. I almost lost Christ in the waves and blasts of despair and blasphemy against God, but God was moved by the prayers of the saints [other Christians] and began to take pity on me and rescued my soul from the lowest hell.[18]

He wrote to another friend, John Agricola, during this time, saying,

> Please do not stop comforting me and praying for me, because
> I am poor and needy. . . . Satan himself rages with his whole
> might within me, and the Lord has put me in his power like
> another Job. The devil tempts me with great infirmity of spirit,
> but through the prayers of the saints I am not left altogether in
> his hands, although the wounds he gives my heart will be hard
> to heal.[19]

Waves of doubt and heartache washed over him. Whatever the thoughts, whatever the whispers of the darkness, Luther knew that he would continue to bear the marks of his depression during this season. It would take him months to recuperate. He described the period to one of his friends as a time of "restlessness and faintheartedness."[20] Months later he wrote to Melanchthon again, "Pray for me, wretched and despised worm that I am, vexed with a spirit of sadness."[21]

And yet he called this experience "school." As horrifying as his psychological state was, as much as he would have preferred death to the doubts and fears attacking his mind, Luther found that the experience taught him something. This trial, as with all others, was a school yard, a training ground. He would say elsewhere that trials make us more sure of doctrine, increase our faith, and teach us Scripture's true meaning.[22] It is because of the dark that we learn the nature of the light. This belief did not tritely diminish the dark's intensity or make light of its pain. But it did train Luther to expect to grow in the midst of trials—and sometimes because of them. This expectation was strong enough that he wrote it down as a reminder in the midst of an intense emotional and spiritual fight: *You are at school.*

It was about this time that Luther wrote his famous hymn "A Mighty Fortress Is Our God."[23] He found great power in singing to remind us of the gospel and fight off the attacks of doubt. These resounding words many of us still sing today carry greater weight when I think of the painful physical and emotional fire behind them.

A mighty fortress is our God,
A good mailcoat and weapon;
He sets us free from ev'ry wrong
That wickedness would bring on.
The old knavish foe,
He means earnest now;
Force and cunning sly
His horrid policy,
On earth there's nothing like him.

'Tis all in vain, do what we can,
Our strength is soon dejected.
But he fights for us, the right man,
By God himself elected.
Ask'st thou who is this?
Jesus Christ it is,
Lord of Hosts alone,
And God but him is none,
So he must win the battle.

And the world with devils swarm,
All gaping to devour us,
We will not fear the smallest harm,
Success is yet before us.
The world's prince accurst,
Let him rage his worst,
No hurt brings about;
His doom it is gone out,
One word can overturn him.

The word they must allow to stand,
Nor any thanks have for it;
He is with us, at our right hand,
With all gifts of His spirit.

If they take our life,
Wealth, name, child, and wife—
Let everything go:
They have no profit so;
The kingdom ours remaineth.[24]

There is a declaration of sure victory in these verses, one that speaks all the more to Luther's faith when we remember he was still caught in the midst of the battle.

FED UP WITH THE WORLD: ACCUMULATING LOSS

There were seasons of Luther's life that were consumed with the normal rhythms of ministry in a revolutionary time. He had his parishioners to care for, his children to play with, his students to teach, letters to write, sermons to preach. Then there were seasons when he was hit hard by an accumulation of trials. Maybe you've experienced seasons like this—those seasons when one sorrow is followed by another.

Several years before his death, Luther's beloved Katie suffered a miscarriage that left her extremely ill—so ill, in fact, that she was unable even to walk for two months.[25] I imagine Luther feared he would also have to suffer the loss of his wife.

Two years later, they would lose a precious member of their family: Martin and Katie's thirteen-year-old daughter, Magdalena, who became extremely ill. Luther stayed by her deathbed, comforting her and pleading in prayer. He reminded her of her Father in heaven, of where she was going. Even with her trusting response, he turned from her and said, "The spirit is willing, but the flesh is weak. I love her very much. If this flesh is so strong, what must the spirit be?"[26]

An onlooker described the scene: "When his daughter was in the agony of death, he fell upon his knees before the bed and, weeping bitterly, prayed that God might save her if it be his will. Thus she gave up the ghost in the arms of her father. Her mother was in the same room but was farther from the bed on account of her grief."[27]

Oh, the raw sorrow in this account. Comforting your child as she eases into death, fully aware, old enough to grasp what is happening to her. Comforting your wife as she weeps with loud sobs, trying to say goodbye to her daughter. And in all this, speaking some truth to yourself, trying to remember the Promise in the midst of tears. Magdalena's death was a heavy emotional blow. The high child-mortality rates of the time did not dull the pain of losing his daughter. Years later, Luther still wrote of mourning and missing her.

Along with these personal trials, Luther's health continued to decline, and political troubles in Germany escalated. He told a friend, "I am tired, and nothing more is in me."[28]

Even this great man, Martin Luther, reached the point of just wanting to be done. He was tired of the pain, tired of the trouble, tired of the sorrow. He was depleted, with nothing left to give. Around this time he told Katie, "I am fed up with the world."[29]

Luther would live for almost four more years, continuing on in faithful ministry in spite of his grief and physical pain. By the time he died, he had spun into motion a religious movement that would forever change European—and Christian—history. In his sermons, treatises, letters, and snippets of conversations, he offered fresh interpretations of Scripture. Anyone today who hails from a Protestant tradition has Luther to thank for its existence.

After Luther's death, a paper was discovered in his room, on which was written his last statement. It was a final testament to his own struggles and to the gospel of grace upon which he'd built his life: "We are beggars. That is true."[30]

FIND FRIENDS AND MAKE MERRY

I remember the ache of loneliness and the fear of my own thoughts during the worst of my depression in my college years. I felt cut off from everyone by a thick insulating layer. Others' voices came as if from a distance, reflecting off the thick walls around my heart and mind. I was trapped in a cold, isolating fog.

Some nights I would pick up my notebook and textbook—probably one of the thick volumes of Norton's literature anthology—slowly climb the stairs, and walk to my friends' apartment, not to talk but just to sit. I craved being in the presence of someone else who was living, breathing, warm, alive. People who cared about me were there, breathing the same air, loving me in the midst of my darkness—and that was enough to keep me going.

At times it felt needy, even pathetic—"just please let me sit in your apartment while you're there." But I was unknowingly following one of Luther's oft-repeated pieces of advice for depression: flee solitude. In seeking out company, I was doing one of the best things I could. Luther would have encouraged me that *this* was fighting.

We have several letters with Luther's guidance for how to survive depression. My favorite of these letters was written to a young man named Jerome Weller, who studied with Luther, lived in his house, and even tutored his children. Feeling depressed, Jerome feared he would give in to despair and perhaps even commit suicide. Luther wrote to him with his advice:

> By all means, flee solitude, for the devil watches and lies in wait for you most of all when you are alone. . . . Therefore, Jerome, joke and play games with my wife and others. In this way you will drive out your diabolical thoughts and take courage. . . .
>
> Be of good courage, therefore, and cast these dreadful thoughts out of your mind. Whenever the devil pesters you with these thoughts, at once seek out the company of men, drink more, joke and jest, or engage in some other form of merriment.[31]

This advice may not be easy to follow. It works against the natural pull of depression to isolate and withdraw. Solitude brought a strange sort of comfort when I was depressed. I didn't have to act normal, didn't have to summon the energy to engage, to make eye contact, to smile, to converse. I could simply be, could simply disappear. But Luther would have told me to fight against this inclination. To not only avoid solitude but flee it. To surround myself with friends, to do anything but remain alone.

Luther knew the chilling isolation of solitude. As he sat in his rooms at Wartburg Castle, he wrestled with dark thoughts alone. He understood that, without the diversion, comfort, and delight that friends offer, we become more vulnerable to our own thought progressions: "The worst and saddest things come to mind. We reflect in detail upon all sorts of evils. And if we have encountered adversity in our lives, we dwell upon it as much as possible, magnify it, think that no one is as unhappy as we are, and imagine the worst possible consequences."[32]

I find Luther's experience so relatable that it brings a morbid smile to my lips. Just as he describes, I have seen depression feed and escalate my negative thought patterns. All sorts of thoughts and memories come to mind: twisted perceptions of myself or those I love, hurt I thought I'd moved past, lies I thought I'd never believe. They string one after another, leading deeper and deeper down into an abyss of hopelessness and self-loathing and spiraling further and further from reason and reality. Being alone allows us to stay in this prison of our own mind, with little to pull us from it. In solitude, these thoughts become more vicious, more convincing, and, sometimes, more dangerous.

To a woman concerned about her suicidal husband, Luther wrote,

> Be very careful not to leave your husband alone for a single moment, and leave nothing lying about with which he might harm himself. Solitude is poison to him. For this reason the devil drives him to it.... Whatever you do, do not leave him alone, and be sure that his surroundings are not so quiet that he sinks into his own thoughts. It does not matter if he becomes angry about this.[33]

Don't be alone, Luther urges. Go find some company.

What about those moments when there aren't friends close by, when there isn't a safe haven to get to? What if you really are isolated? When Luther found himself in this sort of position, he got creative:

> When I am assailed with heavy tribulations, I rush out among my pigs, rather than remain alone by myself. The human heart is like a millstone in a mill . . . if you put no wheat [under it], it still grinds on, but then 'tis itself it grinds and wears away. So the human heart, unless it be occupied with some employment, leaves space for the devil, who wriggles himself in, and brings with him a whole host of evil thoughts, temptations, and tribulations, which grind out the heart.[34]

If you can't be with your friends, go hang out with your pigs, Luther says. Refuse to be alone. Do not allow your darkened thoughts to continue grinding, spinning, swirling in your mind. Find some warm-blooded being, any sort of companionship, to keep your melancholy feelings at bay.

When our inner being is clouded by depression, untethered and drifting, we can't fully trust our own thoughts or perception of reality. Depression has a way of distorting reality, of cloaking lies as truth. Our friends—in Luther's mind, particularly our fellow Christians—can remind us of truth, of reality, of hope. "It is high time that you cease relying on and pursuing your own thoughts," he wrote to a friend. "Listen to other people who are not subject to this temptation. Give the closest attention to what we say, and let our words penetrate to your heart. Thus God will strengthen and comfort you by means of our words."[35]

As the voices of our mind quiet in the safe company of our friends and loved ones, we can begin to listen to their words. They can speak back to us the truth about ourselves and the value of our life, about hope for the future, about their love for us. These truths, and the truth of God's Word, become even more powerful as they enter our ears from their lips. Luther says, "Do not dwell on your own thoughts, but listen to what other people have to say to you. For God has commanded men to comfort their brethren, and it is his will that the afflicted should receive such consolation as God's very own."[36]

I think of Luther's dearest friends and the letters they exchanged, of the conversations that are lost to history. I think of Staupitz, directing Luther's gaze to the cross. I think of the ways they comforted him when his world went dark, of how they bolstered him up.

I also think of his wife Katie. When he was overcome by worries and fears, she comforted him with the words of Scripture. In the most desperate of cases, she employed the dramatic:

> Once, when Martin was so depressed that none of Kate's counsel would help, she put on a black dress. Luther noticed it and asked, "Are you going to a funeral?"
>
> "No," Kate replied, "but since you act as though God is dead, I wanted to join you in your mourning."
>
> Luther got the message and recovered.[37]

It's clear Luther took his own advice and listened to her as if from God himself. He opened his ears to hear the truth she spoke, and acted on it as best he could. Sometimes this brought relief enough to carry on.

Luther went even further in his advice, though. With the friends (or pigs) we've sought out, he said we should find some sort of merriment. Oh what a challenge—to "joke and jest" when the heart is heavy, the world is dark, thoughts clouded. This also flies in the face of depression's nature, which dims the pleasure of everything. But Luther saw embracing life to its fullest possible means and relishing in its delights as a weapon. He calls us to go be among friends, find something to enjoy that will help you relax, and laugh, even if doing so is the hardest struggle.

Writing to a young prince who suffered from depression, Luther suggested that it would be good for him

> to engage in riding and hunting, and to seek the company of others who may be able to rejoice with Your Grace in a godly and honorable way. For solitude and melancholy are poisonous and fatal to all people, and especially to a young man. . . .
>
> Be merry [with your friends at hand]; for gladness and good cheer, when decent and proper, are the best medicine for a young person—indeed, for all people. I myself, who have spent a good part of my life in sorrow and gloom, now seek and find pleasure wherever I can.[38]

Here we find a better context to hear Luther's recommendation for Jerome to "drink more." He was not suggesting that good old Jerome Weller forget his sorrows through drunkenness. Self-medicating with alcohol or other drugs is dangerous—particularly when you're already suffering with a mental illness. Rather, as the letter above to the prince makes clear, Luther is advocating for good, hearty pleasure. I think he's encouraging both of them to relish the simple, physical pleasures of life that do good for our hearts. He's telling them to find something that will provide joy and enjoyment, something that will keep them grounded in the goodness of life.

Sometimes it may feel impossible to summon the energy to engage in these enjoyable things. Sometimes we may feel like we need to reteach ourselves how to smile. Sometimes we may be simply going through the motions, positioning ourselves in these activities and moments to be ready when a sliver of joy may appear. But whether it's riding and hunting, playing music, laughing and joking with friends, or eating and drinking, we seek some source of delight, some physical means of pulling us from our thoughts and reminding us of the goodness in God's world.

Find laughter. Find the smallest glimmers of joy. And chase them.

2

HANNAH ALLEN

Attend to Body, Mind, and Spirit

A sliver of light broke into the darkness of her hiding place. Day. The family would be awake soon. Little did they know she was close enough to hear their movements, to listen to their concerned voices. Were they still searching for her, scanning the woods for her body?

The first day, she feared her stomach would betray her. It rumbled, begging for nourishment. Surely someone could hear. She willed herself to be still, to keep her limbs stiff, her breaths low. She willed her hunger away, embracing the empty void in her gut. As the hours slowly passed, the hunger quieted. She slipped in and out of sleep under the dark cloth that would be her burial shroud. She waited for the end to come.

But the end did not come. After three days, still she lay, hidden under the floorboards. They had been cold days, and the chill had sunk into her bones. Her body trembled and ached—from the cold, from the close quarters. Sensation receded from her fingers and hands. Was this how it felt to be a corpse? Stiff, cold, buried in the dark?

But she was not a corpse. Her breath still came in slow, ragged gasps. Her heart still beat, slow and loud in her chest.

Why didn't life abandon her? She was no longer deserving of it. She was lost, irrevocably, to the devil's schemes. A monster. A wretch removed from God's grace. Death was the only answer.

She thought of her son, of his small, trusting face. How would he cope without his mother, even as poor a mother as she was? She thought of her cousins, of their kindness in keeping her as a guest. How would they feel to find her body hidden in their house?

She was weary of life—but she did not want to die. She wanted to sit by the fire, to feel the warmth of its flames rekindle the blood in her veins. She wanted to see her son and feel his tiny body pressed against her chest.

Her body was weak from hunger, stiff from cold. She did not want to die.

Footsteps echoed along the boards above her face. Someone was coming. With the last of her strength, she cried out.

JOURNALS OF AFFLICTION

Nearly a decade before Hannah Allen's attempts at suicide, she was a young bride of seventeen, happily married to her husband, Hannibal. They joyfully welcomed a son. The cloud over their domestic bliss was Hannibal's frequent absences from their home in England on merchant voyages, which sent Hannah dipping into melancholy.

After eight years of marriage, she received devastating news: Hannibal had died at sea. Hannah suddenly found herself grief stricken, a young widow with a young son to care for alone. She went to live first with her aunt and then with her mother, but the loss of Hannibal precipitated a deeper descent into depression.

In this tenuous place, Hannah fought in the best ways she knew how. She sought medical care but still saw her mental state wreaking havoc on her body and her health. She traveled to see friends, which provided relief but only for as long as she was in their presence. She employed the tools of her faith, repeating promises to herself from

Scripture that applied to her situation. But nothing helped to ward off her growing despair. Her condition only grew worse.

For several years—until her depression grew too debilitating—Hannah recorded her interior and spiritual life in a journal, writing of her struggles and temptations and of the ways she saw God working in them. She also wrote down her prayers. These journals gave her a place to record and process her experiences.

Journaling also helped Hannah remember. As her mental and emotional state declined, she read through her journals from previous struggles and remembered how God had worked in the past. She remembered the years when she had secretly fallen under melancholy's sway as a teenager. She remembered God's intervention in the surprising camaraderie and comfort of a book by a contemporary pastor. She remembered how God had eased her despair.

As I read Hannah's journal entries, her words sound familiar, as if they could be pulled from my own journals during my own depression. She suffers. She wrestles with her thoughts, begging God to intervene, fighting between hope and despair. I can relate to her sense of spiritual isolation, to the fragility of her faith. She writes, "At the first I began to complain that I found not that comfort and refreshment in Prayer as I was wont to do, and that God withdrew his comforting and quickening Presence from me. . . . One hour my hope was firm, and the next hour ready to be overwhelmed."[1]

Oh the energy it took to get out of bed each day, to dress, to care for her child, to eat! It was daunting, drudgery. "Every day at present seems a great burthen [burden] to me," she said.[2] Life stretched on in an endless string of days. It felt like more than she could bear. She begged for strength to endure. She prayed for her trial to somehow be transformed for good. But she found herself at a loss: "I know not what to say; the Lord pity me in every respect and appear for me. . . . I know not what to do, I shall be undone."[3]

A few weeks later, she threw herself on God in desperate dependence:

Lord, I know not what to do, only mine Eyes are up to thee, the Devil still keeps me under dreadful bondage, and in sad distress and wo[e], but blessed be my God, that he doth not lay upon me all afflictions at once; that my Child is so well, and that I have so many other mercies, which the Lord open my Eyes to see; especially that Christ is mine, for the Lord's sake, and then I have enough.[4]

Hannah fought to see God's work in the midst of her struggle. She had nowhere else to turn. She trained her eyes on his blessings, perceiving how things could be worse. And she prayed for open eyes to see Christ's presence and promise of salvation as "enough."

This, for a brief time, seemed to help her, as it has helped me when depression is mild and hasn't taken complete control. But these practices do not create an impenetrable wall, and Hannah found depression continuing to chip away at her mind and her faith. This would be her last entry, as her condition worsened and she lost sight of even the hope of salvation.

"MONSTER OF THE CREATION": HANNAH'S SPIRITUAL DELUSIONS

Depression notoriously seeps into our spiritual lives. (I have yet to meet anyone for whom this isn't the case.) Thoughts grow sluggish, prayers leaden. It can feel as though God's presence has silently withdrawn, leaving us behind in a foggy mist of doubt, fear, and desperation.

It should come as no surprise, then, that Hannah's depression came with intense spiritual struggles. Her spiritual life didn't just come under depression's sway, however, as many of us have experienced; it also became an obsession that clouded and deluded her mind.

She wasn't alone. Many others suffered from what was then called "religious melancholy,"[5] though we'll never read their stories. They are the silent sufferers lost to history.

This is why Hannah's story is important, even though she did not influence a monumental shift in church history like Martin Luther or write still-loved sermons or hymns like Charles Spurgeon or William Cowper. Hers is the story of an everyday Christian trying to live faithfully in the midst of the trials of life, but the history of the church is built on the lives of "normal" people like her. Her struggle is no less significant because few know her name. Neither are the struggles of the other brothers and sisters who battled (and battle) depression, though we may never know their names in this life. We need stories like Hannah's—we need *your* story—because we see God's faithfulness and handiwork in them just as much as in those of our heroes.

Hannah's pain casts a shadowy outline of what others who were afflicted with "religious melancholy" may have experienced. It is depression with a decidedly religious fixation. Assaulted by what she called temptations from the devil, she was so overwhelmed by her sense of guilt and sin that she came to believe she was an unparalleled sinner. She read and repeated parts of the Bible in a way that twisted them to apply judgment to herself. Words intended to be a comfort became a curse. Over time, she believed "the Devil had overcome [her] irrecoverably," and all was lost.[6] She insisted God had revealed her damnation. Human voices appeared to her to be devils disguised as men, rejoicing in her downfall. She declared she was "a Terrour to my self and all my Friends; that I was a Hell upon Earth, and a Devil incarnate."[7] No one could persuade her otherwise.

Ministers and friends came to visit. They offered to pray with her, to preach to her. They offered spiritual comfort. But to no avail. She avoided going to hear the Word of God (in sermons) or taking the sacrament of Lord's Supper because she thought they would only heap more condemnation and guilt on her. She told them she wasn't to be prayed for.

When they continued to try to persuade her of the error of her thoughts, she had a rebuttal for every point. For instance, they went along with her insistence on the devil's control over her but told her stories of people freed from demon possession through prayer. Demon possession would be favorable compared to her state, she told them, for it could be remedied. She was "a thousand times worse than the Devil" and the "Monster of the Creation."[8] Her sins were so great that "the Devil himself was a Saint" compared to her. When they reminded her of the gospel and of the offer of the forgiveness of sins, she insisted she could not be forgiven and was lost eternally.[9] It's tragic to hear her deluded thoughts. It's frustrating to see her stubborn yet misguided logic. She began to etch on the walls with her scissors: *"Woe, Woe, Woe and alass to all Eternity; I am undone, undone for ever, so as never any was before me."*[10]

Hannah expressed a desire to see only one spiritual advisor during this season: Richard Baxter. His opinion and assessment of her spiritual condition was one she would trust. This is where my historical imagination sparks. When had she heard of this Puritan pastor? How had she learned of his compassionate care for those under melancholy's sway?

Sadly, Hannah and Baxter never met. Hannah's cousin tried to arrange a meeting between them, but despite his best efforts he was never able to manage it. Based on a sermon Baxter preached years later titled "The Cure of Melancholy and Overmuch Sorrow,"[11] however, I can imagine he would have told her something along these lines:

"You aren't alone in these feelings—no matter how much you may feel that you are the only one who has felt this way, that you are the worst sinner on the face of creation. The fact that you hate these thoughts and loathe these feelings is a sign they are the devil's temptations, not of God and not the true state of your soul.

"These feelings arise from the dysfunction of your body, a state just as real as a broken leg. Find a doctor skilled in treating melancholy and obey his medical advice. You cannot trust your troubling thoughts—instead trust the words and truths spoken to you by those 'more right-headed than you are now,' even if you can't fully believe them yourself. Don't dwell on these thoughts or spend too much time musing. Put your mind to rest, turn it to different thoughts, and don't be idle.

"Don't be alone. Now is not the time for solitude or for long private prayers and meditations. Keep to the company of the friends and family who care deeply for you, pray in the company of the body of the church. Let them remind you that God's love is for you. And as you can, comfort others with the comfort you have received through this trial. It will remind you that yours is not the only mind to suffer. In comforting them, you will preach to yourself, and you will solidify the truth in your soul."

SMOKING SPIDERS: SUICIDE AND STARVATION

When Hannah's depression first intensified, she was convinced of her imminent death. Every morning, she declared that she would die before evening and every night that she would die before morning. Her aunt and mother determined they should move her to London, where she could receive better care "both for Soul and Body." Hannah, however, insisted she would die on the journey.[12] Even after they persuaded her to go to London, she struggled to get out of bed each morning throughout the trip: "I would earnestly argue against it, and say, *I shall surely dye by the way, and had I not better dye in bed? Mother, do you think people will like to have a dead Corps in the Coach with them?*"[13]

Eventually, Hannah began to believe that a natural death was too merciful for her depraved state. God was singling her out for a particularly horrific end, she surmised. It was yet another of her delusions, and it became a deadly one. This was when she began to think of ending her own life.

After Hannah did in fact survive the trip to London, her mother settled her into her brother's house and returned home. Her unmarried brother was often away on business, so Hannah found herself too often alone, with only a couple of her brother's servants in the house. This gave her unhealthy amounts of time to ruminate over her dark thoughts—exactly what Baxter would have warned her about—and too much time to contemplate and plan how she would attempt to snuff out her existence.

She sent the maid to the apothecary for opium, but the maid returned empty-handed, telling Hannah either that the shop didn't have opium or that they refused to give it to her because of how dangerous it was. I wonder if this was true or if it was the lie of a tender-hearted woman who was trying to keep a deadly drug out of the hands of a mistress whose mind was unmoored and desperate for an end to her suffering.

Hannah's suicidal ideations then took a morbidly creative turn. She began to catch spiders, which she believed to be poisonous. (As far as I can tell, there were no spiders anywhere in England poisonous enough to have caused Hannah any harm.) She put them in her pipe with a little tobacco and smoked them, thinking she could poison herself. One night, after smoking a spider before bed, she awoke, convinced she was dying. Suddenly fearful at the prospect of death, she called her brother and told him what she'd done. He sent for an apothecary, who prescribed a drug to expel any poison. Clearly she was, as Baxter described, "weary of living and afraid of dying."[14]

Her brother, now aware of her suicide attempts, knew Hannah couldn't be left alone. In her current state, she needed more care and observation than he could give. After consulting with other family members, he sent Hannah to live with the Walkers. Mrs. Walker was a relative, and Hannah says she "received me very courteously, though I was at that time but an uncomfortable Guest."[15] I do not discount the generosity and kindness of this family in welcoming Hannah as a house guest in the state she was in.

Even with the change of scenery and more company and supervision, however, Hannah's suicidal thoughts did not cease. Neither did her attempts on her life. As Hannah reflected on this time in her memoir, she credited God for saving her life: "The watchful Eye of the Lord always graciously prevented me [from the ways] I thought to put an End to my Life."[16] She would later be thankful for this.

While she lived with the Walkers, Hannah also began to starve herself.[17] At first, it seems this was another attempt at suicide. It was at the Walkers' house that she hid herself under the floorboards to slowly meet her end. Over time, Hannah's anorexic behavior only continued to worsen. She went to live with her Aunt Wilson in such a state that she "would not eat sufficient to support Nature."[18] As Hannah herself observed, "I was exceeding Lean; and at last nothing but Skin and Bones." A neighbor, catching sight of her declared, "She cannot live, she hath death in her face."[19]

I can only imagine how difficult it must have been for Hannah's aunt to watch her slowly wasting away. She didn't know how to bear the horrible things Hannah would say either. When Hannah was in a good enough humor to converse, her aunt would try to reason with her, to convince her that her thoughts were delusions and thus wrong. "But when she began to speak with me of such things," Hannah wrote, "I would generally fling away in a great fume, and say; *Will you not let me alone yet, me thinks you might let me have a little quiet while I am out of Hell.*"[20]

At other times, Hannah broke down in uncontrollable weeping. She said to her aunt, "Oh, you little know what a dismal dark condition I am in."[21]

BY DEGREES: RECOVERY WITH THE SHORTHOSES

After three years of struggle, Hannah's relatives, Mr. and Mrs. Shorthose, came for a visit. As she had done with so many, she refused to see them. Even when they were under the same roof, dining with her Aunt Wilson, Hannah secluded herself. The Shorthoses understandably only grew more concerned by Hannah's isolation.

The next night, they dined with Aunt Wilson again, this time at the home of a mutual relative. After dinner, they stole away from the rest of the group and secretly went to the Wilsons' house. Knowing that Hannah was unwell, they felt they had to see her. When they slipped in through the back door and entered the kitchen, they found a startled and irate Hannah. She ran to the large fireplace and brandished the tongs, screaming about her aunt's betrayal, whom she assumed had acted against her wishes. After assuring her that her Aunt Wilson knew nothing of their presence, the Shorthoses were able to calm her down. Mr. Shorthose took her by the hand, saying, "Come, come, lay down those Tongs and go with us into the Parlour." She relented, and after a long conversation, they left her in such a calm mood that as they departed she said, "I am loth to part with them."[22]

Encouraged by their encounter, Mr. Shorthose returned the next day and took Hannah for a walk. By the end of the day, he and her aunt persuaded her to come stay with them. Mr. Shorthose had training not only as a minister but also in medicine. Guided by his own experience and by consultations with other doctors, he put Hannah on a strict course of medical treatment throughout the summer. Under his care, she finally began to show improvement. By autumn, when she returned to her family in Snelston, Hannah was once again visiting with friends and attending worship services. Her recovery continued over the next two years. The light dawned slowly, "by degrees," just as the darkness had come.

Her story as we know it ends with her second marriage to a widower named Mr. Charles Hatt. Hannah describes him as a God-fearing man with whom she lived comfortably. It is a seemingly "happy ending," but the remainder of her life is veiled to us. Most scholars agree she had died by the time her spiritual autobiography was published, about fifteen years later.

BODILY DISTEMPERS AND SPIRITUAL MALADIES: A HOLISTIC VIEW OF DEPRESSION

What fascinates me about Hannah Allen's experience is her insistence on the relationship between her physical and spiritual trials. In this way, her suffering was not unlike Martin Luther's. The physical and spiritual were deeply intertwined, and as one painfully flared, so did the other. In spite of her religious obsessions and the profound religious fixation of her depression, she declared clearly that her body was healed, and the spiritual disturbances worked out as a result:

> as my dark Melancholy bodily distempers abated, so did my spiritual Maladies also, and God convinced me by degrees; that all this was from Satan, his delusions and temptations, working in those dark and black humors, and not from my self, and this God cleared up to me more and more; and accordingly my love to, and delight in Religion, increased.[23]

Hannah would say Satan used her physical state—her mind darkened and corrupted by melancholy—to tempt her soul. But she insisted that it was as her melancholy left her that her spiritual state returned to normal—not the other way around.

I know many people who struggle with the blurring of the line between depression and the spiritual life. Those of us who suffer with depression hear the refrain to "just pray more" or "just have more faith." We're asked how we can be depressed if the fruit of the Spirit includes joy. I once heard someone who was praying for a Christian friend struggling with suicidal thoughts say, "Lord, we know she once knew you but for some reason is choosing to walk away from that right now"—as if her faith had been cast to the wayside instead of being one of the few things keeping her alive.

I have seen great damage done with this mentality. Pain and guilt are compounded. I have felt the burden of that guilt myself—of the shame that I ought to be doing better, ought to be a "better Christian" (whatever that means). And I have sat with the tears and questions of other dear souls who are caught in the crosshairs of these accusations.

Depression is a spiritual issue in the sense that everything in our lives is a spiritual issue—our habits, our thoughts, even the minutest of decisions. But we cannot classify depression as a solely spiritual issue, with solely spiritual causes and a solely spiritual cure—even in a case like Hannah's, where thought patterns were particularly spiritual. Those caring for her in the seventeenth century, far before the development of modern psychology or neuroscience or psychotropic medications, knew the situation was more complicated than that. The anonymous writer of the introduction to her autobiography reminds us that "if the Body be out of frame and tune, the Soul cannot be well at ease."[24]

Sure, her friends tried to persuade her to reason. They prayed with her. They continued to remind her of the truth of her faith. These actions are part of the arsenal of the Christian community in the midst of all sorts of painful circumstances. They are the means by which the community of faith surrounds its walking wounded, whether that "wound" is depression or any other malady that may befall us. But the importance of prayer or the encouragement of Scripture does not mean we can abandon other means of healing. We wouldn't do it for cancer. We can't do it for depression either.

Hannah and her faithful caretakers remind us that we must treat depression holistically. We seek the healing of body, mind, and soul. We care for the soul, battered about by depression's wiles. And we use the medical options available, like evidence-based therapies and medication. These actions should not be mutually exclusive.

The cure for Hannah Allen wasn't to drag her to church. It wasn't to convince her to pray more. It wasn't to quote Scripture at her until it removed her despair. Her caretakers sought for her the best medical care of the day. They changed her surroundings. They put her on what we would now call suicide watch. They kept showing up with compassion. They attended to her soul, yes, but they also attended to her body.

Was God still at work? Absolutely. Hannah tells us herself that God, in his mercy, was still with her in her darkest days. He was still present and working in the pain. But this didn't stop her from seeing a doctor.

3

DAVID BRAINERD

Leave a Legacy of Faithful Weakness

With each passing hour, civilization slipped farther behind him. He must have passed into New York by now.

He thought of his brother John, walking the halls of Yale, and longed to be with him. He thought back to his own days in those rooms—praying with his friends, meeting with tutors. How different his life would be if he had learned self-control, if he had tempered his pride, curbed his tongue, resisted partisan zeal. He would be nearly finished with his degree, ready to pour his care into a parish as a simple minister. But here he was, edging farther and farther into a howling wilderness.

Creation seemed dead, caught in late-winter purgatory, the trees towering skeletons. As he absently stared at the gradations of gray slipping past, his horse's footfalls thudded in chorus with his heartbeat. It was the sound of a hammer resolutely driving in the nails of his coffin.

He thought of his father, that dignified presence whose face was hazy in his childhood memory. The well-worn image of his mother's face came to mind as well, bringing with it memories of the yeasty smell of her warm kitchen. He remembered the way his proud adolescent composure dissolved into secret tears in the dark of night after they planted her in the earth. There was his brother Nehemiah, too, and the two young children he had left behind when the bloody cough of consumption strangled the last of his breath. He thought of all the people he'd buried.

How he envied them. They were free of this world, with its inexpressible and unstoppable sorrow. It was a vacuum, a gaping emptiness that devoured all joy, all pleasure. He was weary of it. How much longer must he wait for death to steal him away?

He tried to pray, but he could not formulate the words. His thoughts were unruly and sluggish. There seemed to be no God to go to. Had he sent him into this gloom and then left him? Would he withdraw his mercy forever? Would death bring relief if he were lucky enough for it to find him, or would he find himself apart from grace? The thoughts came like unrelenting waves, billowing with doubt and dejection, crashing over his mind, pressing him under, threatening to drown him. He thrashed against them, his heart screaming for peace, for stillness, for clarity. The more he thought, the deeper his mind sank—numb, paralyzed, adrift.

Perhaps this had been a mistake. Who was he to be a preacher of the gospel? What success could possibly come of his mission? He was ignorant. Weak. Helpless. Unworthy. A vile thing, unfit to walk God's earth. The task ahead was beyond his feeble abilities.

The horse plodded on, and he did not change her course. Go rather than stay, he had said to himself in the months before. *I will go rather than stay. God help me.*

COLLEGE RADICAL TURNED MISSIONARY

As David Brainerd's horse trotted along the roads to his first post in upper New York, he was far from what we idealize as the perfect missionary. In the months leading up to his journey, he wrote,

> My spiritual conflicts to-day were unspeakably dreadful, heavier than the mountains and overflowing floods. I seemed enclosed,

as it were, in hell itself: I was deprived of all sense of God, even of the being of a God; and that was my misery.... My soul was in such anguish I could not eat; but felt as I suppose a poor wretch would that is just going to the place of execution.[1]

He wasn't riding a spiritual high, confident in his abilities, secure in his spiritual life. God felt distant, and he felt inadequate. The weight of his new endeavor settled on him like a noose. He fought for any semblance of joy. He was depressed.

It is impossible to read through the words of Brainerd's diary and not notice his depression. Jonathan Edwards, who edited *The Life and Diary of David Brainerd* after Brainerd's death, felt the need to mention it explicitly in his introduction to it. Even the extensive changes and cuts Edwards made to Brainerd's words couldn't hide his melancholy. It was too prominent. Edwards had no choice but to admit Brainerd's bent toward depression, and he declared it an "imperfection" in him.[2] Brainerd's despair and discouragement play a consistent refrain throughout his years of ministry. You can see it cycling—he'll be desolate and longing for death and then will slowly improve, only to dip back down again. Just as consistent, though, is his determination to continue.

During his travels to his first post, he wrote, "I was evidently throwing myself into all hardships and distresses in my present undertaking. I thought it would be less difficult to lie down in the grave; but yet"—and here is the theme of his life—"I chose to go, rather than stay."[3]

Brainerd "went" in spite of his fears or his feelings and in the face of plaguing doubt and insecurity. He continued on to new missionary posts and kept preaching even when he didn't see results. Constantly on the move, he traveled from settlement to settlement, to meetings and conferences, to small New England towns. In one year alone, toward the end of his ministry, he rode three thousand miles on horseback. He was always going. When depression clouded his vision and tuberculosis eventually sapped his strength, he continued to fight to be faithful to his understanding of God's calling.

That calling hadn't always been to be a missionary in the backwoods of New York, Pennsylvania, and New Jersey. David Brainerd first intended to be a minister, like his grandfather and great-grandfather before him.

He entered Yale at the age of twenty-one, in the midst of the cluster of revivals sweeping through New England later known as the Great Awakening. By Brainerd's third year of college, New Haven and Yale were in an uproar, and the frenzy of religious fervor swept him up as it had so many others. His zeal quickly found him in the office of Yale's rector, Thomas Clap, who was a staunch "Old Light" (against the revivals) and displeased by the threat to order and established norms. Under Clap's leadership, the school instituted a new rule prohibiting any students from speaking poorly of the faculty's spiritual lives. An eavesdropping underclassman reported Brainerd for remarking that one of his tutors, Chauncey Whittelsey, possessed "no more grace than this chair," a comment that essentially called into question Whittelsey's salvation.[4] When Brainerd refused to give a public confession for what he thought to be a private crime, he was expelled.[5]

With his disciplinary fist, Thomas Clap slammed the doors on Brainerd's sense of call and desire to enter the ministry. It wasn't as simple as enrolling in another college—there were not the options available today. Brainerd was devastated. He felt keenly what he perceived to be a disgraceful attack on his character and reputation. He also felt guilty and "vile," and wondered if God would ever find him useful. These feelings continued to plague him even after he began his ministry.[6]

Brainerd eventually mellowed (as did most of the revival preachers during the First Great Awakening), but he never abandoned the experiential warmth of the Awakening. He did, however, reject the extremism and judgmentalism it had fueled—of which he had been a part—and later deeply regretted what he called a "party spirit": this revivalist spirituality that caused such division and contention. He became a mediator for multiple congregations embroiled in similar divisions and was gifted at bringing both sides back into harmonious Christian fellowship. His experience as a "radical" became an aid in this peacemaking.

It did not, however, restore his position at Yale, and it did not award him a degree. Many friends and allies negotiated on his behalf, but he never returned.[7]

Though Brainerd couldn't be a minister without a degree and ordination, in the summer after his expulsion he was licensed by an association of Congregational ministers in Connecticut, which permitted him to preach. Several months later, the Society in Scotland for Propagating Christian Knowledge appointed him as a missionary to the Native Americans. He visited one of the few missionaries already deployed—John Sergeant in Stockbridge, Massachusetts— and then set out on that gloomy road for his appointed post in Kaunaumeek, near present day Albany, New York. He was twenty-five years old.

In a Lonely, Melancholy Desert

Brainerd was raised in a well-respected, established New England family. Though not rich, his family was comfortable and connected. He had spent his days walking through towns and cities, discussing religion in well-appointed drawing rooms. When he reached Kaunaumeek, his genteel lifestyle careened head-on into that of the frontier. About a month after arriving there, Brainerd wrote to his brother John:

> I live in the most lonely melancholy desert, about eighteen miles from Albany. . . . I board with a poor Scotsman; his wife can talk scarcely any English. My diet consists mostly of hasty-pudding, boiled corn, and bread baked in ashes, and sometimes

a little meat and butter. My lodging is a little heap of straw, laid upon some boards, a little way from the ground; for it is a log-room, without any floor, that I lodge in. My work is exceedingly hard and difficult; I travel on foot a mile and half [*sic*] in the worst of roads almost daily, and back again; for I live so far from my Indians. I have not seen an English person this month. These and many other uncomfortable circumstances attend me; and yet my spiritual conflicts and distresses so far exceed all these that I scarce think of them, but feel as if I were entertained in the most sumptuous manner. The Lord grant that I may learn to *endure hardness, as a good soldier of Jesus Christ!*[8]

Over the next four years of his ministry, the complaints never changed. He was lonely. His accommodations were hard on his ailing body, which was already afflicted with the tuberculosis that would claim his life four years later.[9] The Native Americans were scattered and far apart, and the physical distance between his lodging and their settlements made it difficult to meet with them. All around him was a howling wilderness and within him a storm of guilt and fear, discouragement and despair. Just a week after arriving in Kaunaumeek, Brainerd wrote,

Appeared to myself exceeding ignorant, weak, helpless, unworthy, and altogether unequal to my work. It seemed to me I should never do any service or have any success among the Indians. My soul was weary of my life; I longed for deaths beyond measure. When I thought of any godly soul departed, my soul was ready to envy him his privilege, thinking, "Oh, when will my turn come! must it be years first!"[10]

His depression clouded his view of himself, his work, and the value of life itself. The following December, he described the world to his brother as one of "inexpressible sorrow," saying, "I am more weary of life, I think, than ever I was. The whole world appears to

me like a huge vacuum, a vast empty space, whence nothing de-
sirable or satisfactory can possibly be derived."[11] In spite of his
feelings, through all his hardships, he simply tried to endure, to
faithfully continue his work in the world he could only call "a dark,
cloudy mansion."[12]

After three months with the Scotsman, Brainerd built a small
house in the Native American settlement to be closer and more ac-
cessible to them in the mornings and evenings when they were more
often at home. In his new house, he still felt deprived of the "neces-
saries and common comforts of life" and would procure bread from
fifteen to twenty miles away only to find it moldy by the time he
went to eat it.

Brainerd also quickly encountered difficulties in his particular
mission. The White Christians had not endeared themselves to the
Native Americans. Rather, they had swindled and deceived Native
tribes out of the ancestral lands they had dwelt on for generations.
And they were destroying Native communities with alcoholism by
providing "firewater." The Native Americans were rightly suspicious
of Brainerd and desperate to protect the slivered remnants of their
land and culture.

Over time, Brainerd also faced opposition from other settlers,
who spread false rumors about him and questioned his motives.
They were angry at the loss of income from alcohol that occurred
as Brainerd encouraged the Native community to curb their
drinking habits.[13] In addition, they suspected conversion to Christianity, and the education that inevitably followed it, would limit
their ability to trick Native peoples into treaties that did not suit
the tribes' interests. Along with these malicious motives was a
simple fear of otherness—of people who were different from
them—that caused them to imagine Native tribes slitting their
throats while they slept.

As all of us are, David Brainerd was a man of his time, and he
brought with him the same racism and attitudes of cultural

superiority that led to the barbaric treatment of Native Americans. Calling them "children," he thought them lazy, ignorant, and inept to handle secular affairs. He did not understand their values and way of life—so different from his own. And he had no vision for a Native form of Christianity, no vision beyond his own White, Western way of following Christ. He was no noble savior, and we must acknowledge his attitudes for what they were.

When we look at Brainerd's behavior against his cultural backdrop, however, some of his behaviors and attitudes are striking. When he first moved to the settlement at Kaunaumeek, for example, he lived with a Native family in their wigwam while he was building his house. Within a year, he learned their language well enough to pray and sing songs of worship with them in their own tongue. He later felt closer kinship with "his people," his Native brothers and sisters in Christ, than the "heathen" Whites, preferring to sleep outside on the ground with his Native companions than in a boarding house with people who shared his own pale skin color.

He also saw Native converts as fellow believers and welcomed them into full fellowship at the Lord's Table. There were some at the time who wondered if this was even possible. He described the response to his message in his last posting in Crossweeksung, New Jersey, as a revival—an awakening of the sort of Jonathan Edwards's White congregation in Northhampton, Massachusetts. These are little steps, surely, but I can't help but wonder what further transformation could have come to his attitudes and behaviors if his life with the Native Americans hadn't been cut short.

DEAD DOG PREACHER

Brainerd had to wait for these days of revival and converts. They didn't come until the end of his life, and for most of his ministry, he struggled to see results. After about a year at his first post in Kaunaumeek, he entrusted "his people" to the care of John Sergeant in Stockbridge—the frontier missionary with whom he'd briefly trained the year before—and moved on to a new assignment in Pennsylvania on the Delaware River (near modern-day Easton). This second post sent him farther out into a wilderness in which he could never seem to see any beauty.

In the months before he moved, Brainerd received tempting invitations from two congregations to take up their pastorate. It was the sort of position he wanted and had been denied by his expulsion from Yale. They would have provided much-needed respite and care for his tenuous physical and mental health. In spite of this, the commissioners of his missionary society dissuaded him from accepting these invitations, and he submitted, once again choosing "to go rather than stay."

He traveled on horseback through the "desolate and hideous country" to his new post.[14] Although Brainerd's perspective was surely clouded by his depression, he was not alone in finding the forests of Pennsylvania daunting. In the eighteenth century, they were challenging and difficult to travel through. Without the established roads of New England that he was accustomed to, Brainerd would have trekked over fallen trees, unfordable streams, swamps, and all sorts of harrowing dangers for a horse. A familiar gloom settled over his mind.

He wrote in his journal, "My heart sometimes was ready to sink with the thoughts of my work, and going alone in the wilderness, I knew not where."[15] Once again in isolation, he felt cut off from all of humanity: "Felt myself very loose from all the world; all appeared 'vanity and vexation of spirit.' Seemed lonesome and disconsolate, as if I were banished from all mankind, and bereaved of all that is called pleasurable in the world."[16] Not only was he separated from friends and fellow Christians, he felt cut off from God himself, mourning after "the presence of God" and seeming "like a creature banished from his sight!"[17]

I can relate to Brainerd's feelings. I remember the sense of God's absence, the silence of heaven, the seeming futility of spiritual exercises. My prayers felt like an escaped paper in the breeze, aimless, twisting, flimsy. I wondered why God didn't show himself, why I couldn't sense his presence. I felt, as Brainerd did, that "I had no power to pray; but seemed shut out from God."[18] I wondered what I was doing wrong.

The wisdom of my counselor at the time pierced through this desolation: If depression affected my relationships with the friends and loved ones I *could* physically hear and touch, why wouldn't I expect it to affect my relationship with God, whom I could *not* physically hear and touch? It didn't mean he had left or changed but only that depression's dark lens affected the way I perceived him and my ability to feel close to him—just as it did to any other relationship. Depression reaches its skeletal hands into every part of us, including our spiritual lives. It affects our whole selves.

David Brainerd is a real-life example that the oft-used maxim "just pray more" is not a mental health cure-all and that a devoted religious life is not a mental health insurance policy. It is hard to imagine anyone outside of a cloister devoting more time and energy to the spiritual life than Brainerd did. He filled his life with prayer, Scripture-reading, and fasting, but they did not prevent or cure his depression.

Brainerd's spiritual life, I am sure, helped him survive his struggles by giving him motivation to keep going, hope when he felt hopeless, and truth that reigned above his circumstances. But there were also ways in which his spirituality and theology unhelpfully played with his depression and exacerbated his mental health crises.

From his childhood, Brainerd was "highly emotional, unhealthily introspective, over-conscientious, and subject to periods of dark depression."[19] And yet, a mentor advised Brainerd as a young man to "abandon young company and associate [himself] with grave elderly people." To diligently read his Bible and spend "much time every day in secret prayer and other secret duties." To listen to and memorize sermons.[20] Though none of these practices are inherently wrong, the added seriousness, introspection, and solitude of this spirituality were hardly helpful to his propensity toward depression. Brainerd himself admitted that solitude allowed his melancholy to deepen: "I find, though my inward trials were great, and a life of solitude gives them greater advantage to settle, and penetrate to the very inmost recesses of the soul."[21] A mentor more akin to Martin Luther would have benefited him—one who would have urged him to flee the solitude that allowed his thoughts to fester.

It's sometimes difficult to tell when Brainerd was speaking from his depressed state and when he was adopting an accepted mode of spirituality. He was often overwhelmed with a sense of his own "vileness" and inadequacy and felt "too bad to walk on God's earth, or to be treated with kindness by any of his creatures."[22] He called himself an "unworthy worm."[23] He wrote,

> I had the most abasing thoughts of myself. . . . I thought myself the worst wretch that ever lived: it hurt me, and pained my very heart, that anybody should show me any respect. Alas! methought, how sadly they are deceived in me! how miserably would they be disappointed, if they knew my inside! . . . [I] felt such a pressure from a sense of my vileness, ignorance, and unfitness to appear in public, that I was almost overcome with it; my soul was grieved for the congregation; that they should sit there to hear such a dead dog as I preach.[24]

Was he speaking from his theology's accepted and expected sense of humankind's humility before God, a sort of sanctified self-loathing? Were his feelings of guilt coming from a genuine need for repentance? Or was he depressed? The fact that it's impossible to know is concerning.

I would argue that if the spiritual culture we're a part of results in never-ending shame, where we are continually cycling through feelings of worthlessness and guilt with no sense of grace, it's time to reevaluate our spirituality. We do not just need a message of guilt and sorrow over sin. We also need to hear the message that we are God's children and beloved.

When we're depressed, our minds can twist things that would otherwise be neutral or positive into something negative and absolute. We become the worst spouse in the world. We are only destined for failure. No one loves us. These are the sound bites that play in our heads. It's no wonder, then, that as Brainerd slipped into depression, he became increasingly pessimistic about his own abilities and the ways God could use him. He wondered why he was even allowed to live. The spiritual climate of which he was a part did not seem to offer a strong remedy to these feelings. In fact, it only added to his insecurity and guilt.

As he continued from posting to posting and saw no fruit from his labors, he was obsessed with what he perceived to be a lack of results. The revivalist mentality of the day certainly did not help with this, as it suggested that a lack of spiritual response could be the fault of the preacher. This only sent him spiraling further into feelings of guilt and inadequacy. He could think of no greater horror than being found "barren" in God's service. His depression seethed.

He was also obsessed with not wasting a moment, as his deep desire was to be useful in God's service, to bear fruit that would last. At the age of twenty-four, he wrote, "I wanted to wear out my life in his [God's] service, and for his glory."[25] This led him to wish he didn't have to sleep so that he could devote more time to spiritual study or prayer. And he felt guilty when he was so weak that he had to preach sitting down or so ill that he did not even have strength to read or think straight because all he had energy for were what he considered to be "trifles."[26] He wanted to fill every moment with explicitly Christian work and saw no other purpose for living. It's as if T. S. Eliot's bird hovered over his shoulders, chirping, "Redeem the time. Redeem the time." His greatest fear was that he would prove to be unprofitable and barren.

Within several months of beginning at the Forks of the Delaware, he wrote,

> My soul longed exceedingly for death, to be loosed from this dullness and barrenness, and made forever active in the service of God. I seemed to live for nothing, and to do no good: and oh, the burden of such a life! Oh, death, death, my kind friend, hasten, and deliver me from dull mortality, and make me spiritual and vigorous to eternity![27]

As admirable as we may find Brainerd's devotion to serving God, as true as we may find his hope of heaven, and as much as we can debate the appropriateness of some of the spirituality of which he was a part, we cannot miss the tragedy in his voice. He called death his "kind friend" and life a burden, and he saw no reason to continue living on the earth.

Many of us recognize his longing. We know that ache, that weariness. We know the sound of that longing to finally shake off the heaviness and the darkness of our existence. Like Brainerd, we wonder at our usefulness, our legacy. Death seems like a friend that will shepherd us into paradise.

But we cannot lose sight of the tragedy of these thoughts. We must, as Brainerd did, carry on as best we can, even when we aren't sure why it's worth the effort. We must continue to choose life. Because life matters. Your life, my friend, matters. Like David Brainerd, bent and broken over his journal, you may not see the fruit of your labor. Depression may have you blinded to the goodness your life offers to the world and to those around you. But as it was with Brainerd, there is more going on than your eyes can see.

A few months later, Brainerd would confess to being "unsuitably desirous of death," writing, "That which often drove me to this impatient desire of death, was a despair of doing any good in life; and I chose death, rather than a life spent for nothing."[28]

A life spent for nothing. It's Brainerd's worst nightmare.

IN THE TIME OF LEAST HOPE

Brainerd stayed at the Forks of the Delaware for one year, building his second house among a second Native tribe. From his account, he did not see an overwhelming response during this time, but he continued to pray that "God would bow the heavens and come down for their salvation."[29] He longed for their conversion, even as the possibility of it, to his mind, defied reason.

During his time there, his diary reveals some of his deepest depression. That winter he wrote,

> Had the greatest degree of inward anguish that almost ever I endured. I was perfectly overwhelmed, and so confused, that after I began to discourse to the Indians, before I could finish a sentence, sometimes I forgot entirely what I was aiming at; or if, with much difficulty, I had recollected what I had before designed, still it appeared strange, and like something I had long forgotten, and had now but an imperfect remembrance of. I know it was a degree of distraction, occasioned by vapory disorders, melancholy, spiritual desertion.[30]

He couldn't think clearly. His body, steadily being worn down by the effect of tuberculosis, was failing him. It felt like God had left him. He knew only one thing to compare this gloom to: hell. When it eased, he lived in fear of its return.

In spite of this depression, Brainerd experienced some important and beautiful developments during his time at the Forks of the Delaware. First, though the laws in Connecticut barred him from any hope of ordination, the political and ecclesial situation of New York allowed for him to take the step that he had longed for— ordination—a few months after his twenty-sixth birthday. So overwhelmed was he by the "greatness of that charge he was about to receive" that he couldn't sleep the night before the ceremony.[31]

Brainerd also began missionary ventures to the Susquehanna, a land still largely untouched by White settlers. These occasional trips along dangerous, single-file trails, through thick underbrush and towering trees, continued until the end of his ministry.

The most significant event of Brainerd's time at the Forks of the Delaware was the conversion of his translator, Tatamy. Since Brainerd's arrival, Tatamy had proven to be experienced and reliable, but Brainerd often found him frustrating and discouraging, once calling him a "distressing weight and burden."[32] As much as Tatamy wanted his people to "conform to the customs of the Christian world," he didn't care much about experiential religion or "divine truths" and didn't hold much hope that his people would change.[33] It certainly didn't help that this was already the hopeless mental track Brainerd's own mind often walked.

All of this changed when Tatamy was converted. Instead of a discouragement, he became an ally. Where once he merely repeated Brainerd's words, he now was impassioned as he translated, often preaching long after Brainerd finished his sermons.[34] Although Brainerd claimed that these sermon extensions were simply Tatamy reiterating his words, I think it's more likely Tatamy was doing some preaching of his own. Sadly, we'll never read these sermons of one of the first Native evangelists to his own people.

Tatamy and his wife were the first Native brothers and sisters in Christ that Brainerd baptized. He continued with Brainerd when he transitioned to his next post and by all accounts was instrumental to Brainerd's success.

In the months after his twenty-seventh birthday, Brainerd left the Forks of the Delaware and began once again in Crossweeksung, New Jersey. The Lenni Lenape community in Crossweeksung was one of several small, scattered communities that had been part of a great nation, which the English called "the Delaware." Hemmed in on all sides and without access to their ancestral hunting, gathering, or farming lands, they had poor access to food. The White settlers had left their traditional lifestyle shattered.

The small group of women Brainerd met upon his arrival quickly increased in size,[35] and he preached to the growing crowd not with scare tactics but by telling of the "compassions of a dying Saviour."[36] Brainerd described what happened next in the language of a revival.[37] Young and old and people of all backgrounds were caught in its flood. Leaders and small children repented, as did a man who was a "murderer, a Powwow or conjurer, and a notorious drunkard."[38] Transformed lives and behavior gave evidence to genuinely converted souls, as the revival swept through the community and all they invited to hear.

Brainerd stood in awe of the very things he had longed for. It came, he said, "at a time when I had the least hope, and to my apprehension the least rational prospect of success."[39] You can hear his spirits buoying as he writes in his journal. God is working. He is not spiritually impotent. There is fruit.

Less than a month after the beginnings of the revival, Brainerd baptized twenty-five Native converts. By the time he left Crossweeksung, eighty-five baptized members of Brainerd's congregation were receiving Communion, which, based on Brainerd's theology and spiritual practices, meant he believed they were genuinely converted. He had arrived without hope, but he left behind a small church. Even before Brainerd departed, it was a church that prayed and worshiped on its own volition and a church Brainerd called on to join him as fellow evangelists on his trips to the Susquehanna.

As the little Native congregation grew, Brainerd saw the difficulties of remaining in the same place in Crossweeksung. When he had arrived, there had been only a few families, but that number continued to grow. Hedged in by White settlers on every side, the community needed more space. So he devised a plan to move the Native people to Cranberry, New Jersey.

His plans once again reveal the tension in his understanding of and relation to the Native Americans. He sought to be their advocate but could not see what he was asking them to give up and couldn't understand their resistance to assimilating to a White cultural standard. However, after much resistance, the Native community did decide to make the move, and once they agreed, things moved quickly.

Brainerd built his fourth and final house in this new community in Cranberry, but he would not be there long. The tuberculosis that had plagued him since his days at Yale was growing ever more serious. Sometimes he could not get out of bed, couldn't preach, couldn't ride. As his energy deteriorated and his body wasted away, he knew the time had come to leave.

"May I Not Outlive My Usefulness"

Amid many tears, Brainerd said goodbye to his congregation and set out on his horse for New England. He instinctively knew he would not return. I wonder, as he rode through the forests and hills, if he fixed the scenery in his mind, searing it into his memory. Did he reflect on all the times he had ridden this way, crossed this stream, passed through that settlement?

In Northampton, Massachusetts, Jonathan Edwards welcomed him into his family home. As Brainerd grew weaker, Edwards's daughter, Jerusha, cared for him. He died there a few months later. Tuberculosis claimed Jerusha's life only months after Brainerd's death, and she was buried beside him in the family plot.[40]

To the end, even while his health declined, Brainerd fretted over his usefulness to God and exerted himself to do anything still within his physical powers. He wrote and edited some of his previous writings. When he became too weak to hold his pen or to sit up in bed, he enlisted help to continue the work through dictation. He also took time to encourage and direct his many visitors—local ministers, candidates for ministry, his brothers, even Edwards's young children. All the way up until his death, he wanted to "not outlive his usefulness," to use every breath given to him to bring God glory.

Though he was in agonizing pain and sometimes delirious, there are no signs of depression in Brainerd's last days. Edwards says it actually made him "more cheerful; as being glad at the appearance of death's approach."[41]

With each day, it became harder and harder to breathe. His chest was tight, his breaths shallow. Moving the wrong way sent stabbing pains through his lungs. His attempts to breathe made his lungs convulse, and uncontrollable coughing took his little breath away, bringing up vomit or infected pus. He was drowning on dry ground.

He begged his friends to pray for him, that he would not "dishonor God by impatience," that he could endure his pain nobly. The thought of enduring another moment was incomprehensible. He had not expected it to be so painful. "It was another thing to die than people imagined," he told his friends.[42]

Even in this state, with more pain than he thought he could bear, his mind turned toward his beloved congregation. On the last night of his life, he stayed up talking with his brother John about them. After his death, John would be the one to carry on his ministry in Cranberry.

LEAVE A LEGACY OF FAITHFUL WEAKNESS

Reading Brainerd's journals, we see again and again how unqualified and "unprofitable" he felt. Multiple times, he lost hope of God's ability to use him. He wondered why anyone would listen to him preach. He called himself a "barren, unprofitable wretch." He wrote sentiments like this in his journal:

> Was so overwhelmed with dejection, that I knew not how to live. I longed for death exceedingly: my soul was sunk into deep waters, and the floods were ready to drown me. I was so much oppressed, that my soul was in a kind of horror: could not keep my thoughts fixed in prayer, for the space of one minute, without fluttering and distraction; and was exceedingly ashamed that I did not live to God. . . . While I was going

to preach to the Indians, my soul was in anguish; I was so overborne with discouragement, that I despaired of doing any good, and was driven to my wit's end.[43]

And yet he stayed. He kept preaching. He continued to walk into the homes of Native Americans and explain the gospel to them. In spite of his feelings, in spite of the whispers of despair, he stayed and kept working as faithfully as he knew how. There's something admirable in that. I think I would have stayed in bed.

Sometimes, all his work seemed for naught. At other times, he saw God meet him in his weakness. After the passage above, after preaching his sermon, he continued,

> [I] was somewhat encouraged to find, that God enabled me to be faithful once more. . . . In the evening I was refreshed, and enabled to pray, and praise God with composure and affection . . . was willing to live, and longed to do more for God than my weak state of body would admit of. I can do all things through Christ that strengthens me; and by his grace, I am willing to spend and be spent in his service, when I am not thus sunk in dejection, and a kind of despair.[44]

In 1930, a few years shy of the two-hundredth anniversary of his death, one religious historian claimed, "David Brainerd dead was a more potent influence for Indian missions and the missionary cause in general than was David Brainerd alive."[45] And he was right. Though Brainerd's effect on the Native American communities to which he'd dedicated the last years of his life was minimal,[46] his ministry would influence others far removed from him. He just couldn't see this in the midst of his own discouragement, even with the brief spark of revival he witnessed.

When Jonathan Edwards published Brainerd's diaries, he immortalized him. In spite of the significant liberties Edwards took as an editor, we can be thankful he preserved the inner life of this young man who would be otherwise lost to us. Like many who would come after him, Edwards put forward Brainerd as an exemplar of the ideal Christian life.[47] Nearly twenty years later, John Wesley, a prominent Methodist leader in England, edited and reprinted Brainerd's diary on the other side of the pond and touted Brainerd as the ideal preacher.[48] He would later be adopted as the ideal missionary and inspire the likes of William Carey (who has been called the father of modern missions) and Jim Elliot. Standing by Brainerd's grave, Adoniram Judson Gordon said, "I do not hesitate to declare that I am now standing at the fountain head of nineteenth century missions."[49] Each facet of Brainerd's life and identity has been held up as a source of inspiration and encouragement to a new generation of students and ministry leaders and lay believers.

I believe it is Brainerd's endurance, not his success, that has made him a hero to so many. Edwards remarked on this constancy:

> His [Brainerd's] religion was . . . like the steady lights of heaven; that are constant principles of light, though sometimes hid with clouds. [It was not] like a land flood which flows far and wide with a rapid stream, bearing down all afore it, and then dried up; but more like a stream fed by living springs, which though sometimes increased by showers, and at other times diminished by drought, yet is a constant stream.[50]

There's something in his faithful weakness that inspires. He himself couldn't see it. All he could see was discouragement and his own inadequacies. All he could do was fight through his depressed thoughts and his longing for death. All he could do was keep praying, even when he thought God hid his face; keep preaching, even when he wondered why anyone would listen to his words; keep riding through the wilderness, even when he didn't quite know where he was going.

From amid the darkest depression and bodily weakness, Brainerd speaks a word of encouragement to us. "Keep at it," he says. "Even when you feel discouraged. Even when you see no fruit. Even when you wonder if God could possibly use you. Carry on. Keep seeking him. Keep at your ministry."

Brainerd's faithfulness is his greatest legacy. It tells us that in our greatest weakness, in the simple act of putting one foot in front of the other, God can still use us.

4

WILLIAM COWPER

Embrace the Rescue of Art and Friendship

The shadows lengthened. He'd watched a shaft of sunlight slide slowly across the wall throughout the afternoon. It lit up the paper, the wood, the painting hung on the far wall, then receded, leaving darkness in its wake. It traced the steady march of time while he waited. He sat on the stairs, his hands resting on his bent legs.

He was alone with his thoughts and the voices that kept him company. They circled like beasts around their unfortunate prey.

His cousin, Johnson—his host, his benefactor, his friend—had departed early that morning for church. The journey was far, but that was not what kept him home, keeping the hours' watch in the hall. The doors to such a sanctuary had been barred to him long ago.

He thought back to the days before the word had come that gave birth to his despair. He had been happy then, caught up in the bliss of a first love. But that was no more.

The air around him grew cold in the deepening twilight. Why hadn't Johnson come?

Perhaps he wouldn't return today. Perhaps this house would become his grave. Perhaps they would seal the doors and he would slowly waste away in a mansion's sepulcher.

Perhaps they would come for him today. They would find him at last and carry him away to execution and fiery torment. They were coming for him, and he was left stripped of a protector.

His breath quickened and came shallow and heavy. He could feel his heart beating fast under the thin covering of his skin. It was the beat of an executioner's drum.

He heard a dog barking at a distance. It echoed the unheard baying of the beasts that chased him—those spiritual hounds in the night season. But the barking now was not the kind that pursued him, so he was bereft of rest or comfort. It came from the farm at the edge of Johnson's estate. Someone was coming.

Would it be Johnson? Or his doom? He gripped the banister railing as if it was the final anchor to keep him from being dragged away.

He listened carefully. There—it was the familiar sound of Johnson's horse, his familiar call of greeting. He didn't realize he'd been holding his breath. His cravat was damp with sweat.

Upon the Rack: First Depression

In the days when he sat anxiously on the stairs each Sunday, William Cowper was nearly sixty. He'd already written the poems and hymns that would preserve his name as an English writer. Depression, and the delusions that accompanied it, had incapacitated him to the point that he came under the care of his young cousin, John Johnson. But this was the end of the story.

From his own account, and from that of those who knew his family, Cowper inherited a propensity for depression. His brother, John, his only sibling out of seven to survive infancy, suffered from it as well. Cowper was a sensitive child and experienced what he described as a "lowness of spirits, uncommon at my age."[1] The loss of his mother just weeks shy of his sixth birthday, a loss still keenly felt decades later, may have contributed to this,[2] as did being sent far from home to school and the merciless bullying of an older classmate. But Cowper's childhood sensitivity could also have been a sign of his proclivity toward depression from an early age.

Cowper describes his first acute case of depression in a brief yet vivid memoir of his early life. It came during his undergraduate days, when he was in his early twenties and a law student:

> I was struck, not long after my settlement in the Temple, with such a dejection of spirits, as none but they who have felt the same, can have the least conception of. Day and night I was upon the rack, lying down in horror, and rising up in despair. I presently lost all relish for those studies, to which I had before been closely attached; the classics had no longer any charms for me.[3]

He found comfort in the poems of George Herbert and in a set of prayers he wrote for himself, though he was not particularly religious at the time. A trip with some friends to the seaside finally brought some relief. As he sat by the sea, the darkness lifted. He said, "I felt the weight of all my misery taken off; my heart became light and joyful in a moment; I could have wept with transport had I been alone."[4] At first he believed his relief to be God's answer to his prayers but then quickly attributed it merely to the change of scenery. When he got back to London, he burned the prayers he'd been using.

About this time, romance blossomed for Cowper in the graceful form of his cousin, Theodora. They fell deeply in love with each other, and their courtship teemed with the fruits of youthful love— letters, stolen visits, love poetry.[5] They promised marriage—and then her father intervened. We don't know the exact nature of his objections. Their close relation was a concern, as was possibly Cowper's mental health and his lack of wealth. Whatever the reason, Theodora's father forced them to break off their engagement, leaving them both heartbroken.

Theodora never married and, it would seem, never forgot William. Over thirty years after their relationship ended, Cowper began to receive notes and gifts from "Anonymous." Most scholars believe Anonymous was Cowper's long-lost love, Theodora, secretly sending him tokens of her continued affection.[6]

Within a year of his dramatic breakup with Theodora, one of Cowper's dearest friends, William Russell, died tragically. In the aftermath of these heartbreaks, Cowper wrote this poem:

> Doom'd as I am in solitude to waste
> The present moments, and regret the past;
> Depriv'd of ev'ry joy I valued most,
> My friend torn from me, and my mistress lost;
> Call not this gloom I wear, this anxious mien,
> The dull effect of humour, or of spleen![7]

The loss of two people he loved covered Cowper's world in a gloomy haze. He insisted, though, that this depression was not rooted in the morbid temperament of his body ("the effect of spleen") but from his painful life circumstances. He knew enough of himself to differentiate the two.

He recovered from this pain without a significant mental health crisis. But the "black, infernal train" would once again "make cruel inroads on [his] brain"[8] and threaten his sanity—and this time it would not be so easy to recover.

HELL'S HUNGRY MOUTH: SUICIDE, MADNESS, AND GRACE

By the time Cowper graduated and became a new member of the Inner Temple (one of London's professional associations of lawyers and judges), he had spent a large part of his inheritance and was in need of a job.[9] One job in particular caught his eye—the clerk of journals in the House of Lords. Knowing his uncle could get him an appointment if there were a vacancy, he solemnly wished for the man currently occupying the seat to die. When the man did, in fact, die a short time later, Cowper suddenly had a job offer.

What Cowper did not anticipate was the way political tensions at the time would get in the way of a quick and easy job appointment. Members of the opposing party called into question his uncle's ability to appoint Cowper and demanded he undergo a thorough examination before the bar.

Cowper, dreadfully shy and loathe to be the center of attention, claimed, "A thunderbolt would have been as welcome to me."[10] The thought of coming before the House of Lords terrified him. He wrote, "They whose spirits are formed like mine, to whom a public exhibition of themselves, on any occasion, is mortal poison, may have some idea of the horrors of my situation."[11] What if he made a fool of himself? He surely would. He could not go through with it. But quitting would bring disgrace on his uncle and further discredit him. What could he do?

Cowper threw himself into study for the examination, but anxiety overwhelmed him to the point that he couldn't focus on the words he read. Each trip to the office to study was like a walk to an execution.[12]

With pressure mounting, Cowper felt trapped. Depression, slowly building, crashed over him with a vengeance. He withdrew from his friends and shut himself up in his chambers. Desperate for an escape, Cowper became convinced that the only solution to his problems would be to take his own life.

He remembered the day when his father had asked him to read a defense of suicide. As an eleven-year-old, Cowper had argued against it. His father had sat quietly, desperate to find a way to process the recent suicide of a dear friend. Now those arguments came back to him. Even if he had been right as a boy in his defense of life, and even if the Bible were true and taught against suicide, he thought, "misery in hell itself would be more supportable" than his current torture.[13]

On the night before his examination, he made several suicide attempts, but each time, thankfully, something intervened to thwart his plans. Some of these interventions were nothing short of miraculous.

Finally, with poison thrown out the window and deep red marks forming around his neck from near strangulation, he called for his uncle, who told him there was no way he could take the post in his condition. Cowper escaped his examination before the House of Lords, but now he faced even fiercer demons—those of the mind.

His poem "Lines Written During a Period of Insanity" describes his tortured state during this time:

Hatred and vengeance, my eternal portion,
Scarce can endure delay of execution,
Wait, with impatient readiness, to seize my
    Soul in a moment.

Damn'd below Judas: more abhorr'd than he was,
Who for a few pence sold his holy Master.
Twice betrayed Jesus me, the last delinquent,
    Deems the profanest.

Man disavows, and Deity disowns me:
Hell might afford my miseries a shelter;
Therefore hell keeps her ever hungry mouths all
    Bolted against me.

Hard lot! encompass'd with a thousand dangers;
Weary, faint, trembling with a thousand terrors;
I'm called, if vanquish'd, to receive a sentence
    Worse than Abiram's.

Him the vindictive rod of angry justice
Sent quick and howling to the centre headlong;
I, fed with judgment, in a fleshly tomb, am
    Buried above ground.[14]

"Buried above ground." I know of few better metaphors to describe what depression feels like.

Cowper lay in bed, terrified of death and of not dying. He felt sure everyone mocked him in the street. He ate dinner alone, hidden in the corner. His friends stopped showing up. Many of these friendships would never be regained. Nightmares haunted elusive sleep.

Then the voices started. They said he was guilty of an unpardonable sin. They said there was no hope. He was under God's wrath. Life was only valuable as a brief stay on God's judgment and the fires of hell. His thoughts became "wild and incoherent," caught in a "strange and horrible darkness." His brain physically hurt.[15]

His brother was in the room to see this transformation and descent into madness as Cowper's mind broke with reality. John took him to a small mental asylum called St. Alban's, which was run by a kind Christian man named Dr. Cotton. Cowper was fortunate to not end up in Bedlam, the infamous mental asylum of the day, and a horrible place. At St. Alban's, he was one of only a few patients, under the compassionate and competent care of Dr. Cotton. But still the depression and the delusions continued. "Eat and drink, for tomorrow thou shalt be in hell" became his mantra.[16]

After about seven months in Dr. Cotton's care, Cowper had a visit from John. He did not find heartening signs of improvement. Cowper declared he was "as much better as despair can make me."[17] Seeing his brother's continued belief he was outside of God's mercy, John launched into a strong argument to convince Cowper it was a delusion. Miraculously, his words broke through the gloom imprisoning Cowper's mind: "Something like a ray of hope was shot into my heart. . . . Something seemed to whisper to me every moment, 'Still there is mercy.'"[18] For the first time, Cowper began to show a little improvement. Life began to hold a little delight.

A few days later, he found a Bible opened to the book of Romans.[19] As Cowper read Paul's words in Romans 3, something within him stirred: "In a moment I believed, and received the gospel.... Unless the Almighty arm had been under me, I think I should have died with gratitude and joy.... I could only look up to heaven in silent fear, overwhelmed with love and wonder."[20] Sleep still evaded him, but now it was because of his profound joy.

Dr. Cotton closely monitored him, fearful that his sudden emotional change was just another part of his mental illness and that it might crash in a "fatal frenzy."[21] Eventually, though, Cowper's demeanor convinced him of a sincere conversion and genuine mental cure. Cowper stayed with him another year after this recovery, and the two men conversed often about their mutual faith.

Shortly after Cowper left St. Alban's, he wrote a letter to his beloved cousin and frequent correspondent, Lady Hesketh, expressing his thankfulness that his mental breakdown brought him to God: "My affliction has taught me a road to happiness which without it I should never have found; and I know, and have experience of it every day, that the mercy of God, to him who believes himself the object of it, is more than sufficient to compensate for the loss of every other blessing."[22]

Cowper's newfound faith and embrace of the gospel played a significant role in pulling him from this first deep depressive episode. The message of God's love for him and of God's mercy was the salve his mind and heart needed. We can rejoice with him in this, even if it isn't the case for all of us. We need only look at the rest of Cowper's life to see that, though in this instance his spiritual life and conversion were a "cure" for his depression, they did not solve everything, and would not be the solution to his recurring depression in the future.

MYSTERIOUS WAYS: THE DEPRESSED HYMNIST OF OLNEY

Cowper left Dr. Cotton and St. Alban's determined never to return to the chaos of London. His brother arranged for him to live in Huntingdon. Though lonely at first, "a traveler in the midst of an inhospitable desert,"[23] he soon met the Unwin family and moved into their home as a boarder.

William Unwin, the son, became like a brother to Cowper and a lifelong friend. Mrs. Unwin, only a few years his senior, became like a second mother. For over thirty years, she was his devoted companion, friend, and caretaker during his seasons of depression. Permanently absorbed into the family, Cowper stayed when Mr. Unwin died suddenly two years later.

Shortly after Mr. Unwin's death, Mrs. Unwin and Cowper met a dedicated pastor named John Newton. Seeking to sit under his spiritual guidance, they moved to his parish in Olney, to a house called Orchard Side, and made a home there for the next twenty years. A path led from their home through the orchard to a small gate at the Newtons' home. As William's friendship with John and Mary Newton deepened, the path became well-worn by exchanged visits. There was hardly a day when they didn't see each other. This was one of the happiest seasons of Cowper's life.

At Huntingdon and Olney, he lived the quiet life of a recluse. His life was simple, and his shy and sensitive nature relished the seclusion of these small towns and their surrounding countrysides. He spent hours walking through the woods and fields and staring at the River Ouse. We see the images of his walks and quiet retirement throughout his poetry. While at times, it certainly did bring him delight, he also says, "It is the place of all the world I love the most, not for any happiness it affords me, but because here I can be miserable with most convenience to myself and with the least disturbance to others."[24]

Although he did not plunge to the same depths as before, Cowper's depression still ebbed and flowed. John Newton, seeking to find something to keep Cowper occupied, suggested they write a collection of hymns. One of Newton's contributions to *Olney Hymns* became the most famous hymn of all time—"Amazing Grace." Cowper penned over sixty hymns for the volume, some of which still appear in hymn books today, such as the one that begins, "There is a fountain, filled with blood, drawn from Immanuel's veins; and sinners, plunged beneath that flood, lose all their guilty stains."

Did Cowper think back on his time in the asylum as he wrote? Did his mind sift through the memories of his many attempts to end his life? Did he rejoice afresh over the "redeeming love" that found him?

One winter, Cowper returned after one of his country walks to write another hymn. He could not shake a premonition of depression's insanity returning in earnest. Ten years had passed since the episode that sent him to St. Alban's. As I read his words, I see him clinging to faith, preaching to himself.

> God moves in a mysterious way
> His wonders to perform;
> He plants his footsteps in the sea,
> And rides upon the storm.
>
> Deep in unfathomable mines
> Of never-failing skill,
> He treasures up his bright designs,
> And works his sovereign will.
>
> Ye fearful saints, fresh courage take,
> The clouds ye so much dread
> Are big with mercy, and shall break
> In blessings on your head!
>
> Judge not the Lord by feeble sense,
> But trust him for his grace:
> Behind a frowning providence
> He hides a smiling face.
>
> His purposes will ripen fast,
> Unfolding every hour;
> The bud may have a bitter taste,
> But sweet will be the flower.

Blind unbelief is sure to err,
And scan his work in vain:
God is his own interpreter,
And he will make it plain!

This hymn, "Light Shining Out of Darkness," introduced the phrase that we now hear more often as "God works in mysterious ways." I hear it often used now in a glib manner, but I wonder if we would consider and use this cliché differently if we remembered it in the context from which it came. Cowper's life and the impending depression he felt as he wrote this hymn add a richer, more faith-filled tenor to the phrase. God works in mysterious ways, indeed, but sometimes this comes through pain and unanswered questions in which we can only trust him to be the "interpreter."

It was the last hymn Cowper would ever write, and his last creative work for nearly seven years. Shortly after, Cowper descended into an "unfathomable mine" from which he would never fully recover, and he would lose the sense of God's "smiling face" for the rest of his life. Truly, God alone would be the interpreter to the despondency he would taste, and Cowper never had the luxury of hearing it this side of the grave.

As depression once again settled into his bones, Cowper quickly lost touch with reality.

I was suddenly reduced from my wonted rate of understanding to an almost childish imbecility. I did not indeed lose my senses, but I lost the power to exercise them. I could return a rational answer even to a difficult question, but a question was necessary, or I never spoke at all. This state of mind was accompanied, as I suppose it to be in most instances of the kind, with misapprehension of things and persons that made me a very untractable patient. I believed that every body hated me, and that Mrs. Unwin hated me most of all; was convinced that all my food was poisoned, together with ten thousand megrims of the same stamp. . . . At the same time that I was convinced of Mrs. Unwin's aversion to me, I could endure no other companion.[25]

After months of refusing to leave the house, Cowper one day made the familiar walk through the orchard to the Newtons' home. He didn't leave for eighteen months. After futile attempts to convince him to return to their own home, Mrs. Unwin moved in as well to care for him. Newton held out hope for Cowper's recovery and willingly loved and cared for him also.[26] He longed for his healing and the return of his sanity—both for Cowper's sake and his own:

> The Lord evidently sent him to Olney, where he has been a blessing to many, a great blessing to myself. The Lord has numbered the days in which I am appointed to wait upon him in this dark valley, and He has given us such a love to him both as a believer and as a friend, that I am not weary; but to be sure, his deliverance would be to me one of the greatest blessings my thoughts can conceive.[27]

John and Mary saw a slow improvement in Cowper's mood and decided to take a trip to Warwickshire. The long-distance medical care of Dr. Cotton convinced them he could be left alone. They did not know of Cowper's latest delusion, however. He believed he had been told the will of God: God wanted him to offer a sacrifice like Abraham, but instead of offering a son, he was to offer up himself. While they were gone, he attempted suicide, sadly believing himself to be committing an act of obedience and dedication to God. Fortunately, he was found and his life spared. John and Mary rushed home as soon as they received the news. They did not leave him alone again, until he left their house just as suddenly as he'd come, with his reason mostly intact.

This episode and this particular delusion haunted Cowper for the rest of his life. Shortly after his suicide attempt, he believed he heard a "word" from God in a dream. Though we don't know exactly what the message was, Cowper summarized it later as, "Actum est de te, periisti": "It is all over with thee, thou hast perished." Cowper understood it to be a promise of his irretrievable loss of God's grace, sealing his fate as one of the damned, all in response to his failure to demonstrate his total obedience to God's "command" to end his life.

Cowper never shook this belief or its accompanying hopelessness. About ten years later, we hear it in a letter to John Newton on the occasion of the new year:

> I looked back upon ... [the old year], as a traveller looks back upon a wilderness, through which he has passed with weariness and sorrow of heart, reaping no other fruit of his labour than the poor consolation that, dreary as the desert was, he has left it all behind him. The traveller would find even this comfort considerably lessened, if, as soon as he had passed one wilderness, another of equal length, and equally desolate, should expect him. . . . I should rejoice indeed that the old year is over and gone, if I had not every reason to prophesy a new one similar to it. . . . [Not one event of the New Year] comes as a messenger of good to me. If even death itself should be of the number, he is no friend of mine. . . . Loaded as my life is with despair, I have no such comfort as would result from a supposed probability of better things to come when it once ended. For, more unhappy than the traveller with whom I set out, pass through what difficulties I may, through whatever dangers and afflictions, I am not a whit the nearer home, unless a dungeon may be called so.[28]

He looked on his life as a steady drudgery. Hope had abandoned him on earth. It would abandon him in the hereafter. I cannot imagine such despair. The fixed surety of his belief makes my heart weep.

Newton and Cowper's other friends held on to hope, even while Cowper could not. They tried to persuade him to believe otherwise.

They reminded him of the gospel. They employed Scripture. They attributed these beliefs to a delusion. But to no avail. Cowper's New Year's letter continues, "You will tell me that this cold gloom will be succeeded by a cheerful spring, and endeavor to encourage me to hope for a spiritual change resembling it;—but it will be lost labour. Nature revives again; but a soul once slain lives no more."[29]

Cowper believed the gospel to be true. He would remind others of its truths and offer them beautiful words of encouragement. We see this repeatedly in his letters. He also knew his friends thought the reasons for his despair were unfounded, but he still didn't think the gospel was true for him.

He stopped praying because he believed it to be in violation of God's will. At meals, he sat while grace was said, his knife and fork in hand, staunchly declaring he had no part in the activity. Neither did he darken the door of a church because he felt it would only incur further wrath against him. He did these things out of what he perceived to be submission to the will of God. God is sovereign. He must obey. He must submit to his own exclusion from grace: "God's ways are mysterious, and He giveth no account of His matters. . . . There is a mystery in my destruction, and in time it shall be explained."[30]

Whereas earlier in his life this belief in God's sovereignty might have brought him hope, he admitted later in life that in some moments, it made him feel "a wish that I had never been, a wonder that I am, and an ardent but hopeless desire not to be."[31]

He lived with this despair for the last twenty years of his life. This gnawing, unabating hopelessness convinced Cowper that God's love was not for him. It makes his story the saddest in this book.

Some of us, by God's grace, find relief from depression for long stretches of time. For others, like our friend William Cowper, it is a never-ending specter. We often hear stories of healing and "victory," of the "Black Dog" in the past tense. But we need to hear stories of "not yet" as well. This is why Cowper's story is so important, though it is tragic and hard to hear. It is a story of the steady, sustaining, unseen work of God—even in one who was convinced God had left him. It's a story about finding pockets of joy and purpose in the presence of chronic depression. It's a story of survival. It's a story of faith with no sight.

At the end of his life, in a season afflicted with nightmares, Cowper shared a dream with a glimmer of this faith: "I dreamed about four nights ago that, walking I know not where, I suddenly found my thoughts drawn toward God, when I looked upward and exclaimed, 'I love Thee even now more than many who see Thee daily.'"[32] Oh, to have such faith.

He could not "see" God's ways. He did not even believe God still loved him. Yet his faith persisted. His love for God persisted in the dark.

We need these stories that refuse to let us jump to a happy ending. We need them to freeze us in the aching tension of the "not yet." We must sit with this pain, bear witness to it, and keep vigil for the yet-to-come redemption.

THE BEST REMEDY: THE ESCAPE OF POETRY

After Cowper's second mental breakdown, he was depressed to some extent for the rest of his life. This ongoing, mild to moderate depression was punctuated by specific episodes of severe depression in which Cowper could not function, experienced psychosis, and several times attempted suicide.

January, in particular, was a dreaded month. It was the month in which his depression returned while at Olney, and the month in which the darkness settled over him and he lost forever a sense of God's favor. He feared it as a portent of doom but also found ways to endure it, day by day, night by night, even when it felt he lived "from hand to mouth."[33]

Cowper found medications that helped his physical and mental ailments.[34] Laudanum helped him sleep. Bleeding was intended to restore the balance of his humors. A variety of barks and powders addressed his headaches and moods. The options were hardly as sophisticated as the medical options we possess today, but Cowper employed what was available to him to keep himself as healthy as possible physically and mentally.

He also developed a deep self-awareness of his need to keep busy. "Amusements are necessary," he once told William Unwin.[35] He had to find ways to stay occupied to pull himself out of his depressive thoughts, away from the soundtrack of melancholy playing on repeat in his mind.

In spite of his best efforts, he still succumbed to seasons when the depression was so deep, so all-consuming, that he couldn't leave the house. He would sit, silent, his hands still, his body frozen. But as soon as he showed the smallest improvement, he began to do something, and these activities were both signs of and partners in his recovery.

He took up hobbies and threw himself into them with gusto.[36] He gardened. He learned to draw. He cared for his many pet animals, which at one time included three tame hares, Puss, Tiney, and Bess, that lived in his house. He learned carpentry and built things, including birdhouses and boxes for his pets. I love to think of him playing with his rabbits in the parlor or of the quiet companionship of his dog Beau as he walked.

Cowper also knew the value of exercise and tried to make time each day for fresh air and moving his limbs. At each of the places he and Mrs. Unwin took up residence, he walked obsessively. And, having experienced the therapeutic benefits of exercise and of the sights of the outdoors for his mental state, he urged others who struggled to also employ them. "Easy chairs are no friends to cheerfulness," he would say.[37]

As Cowper's amusements came and went, one remained as a steady lifeline. Above all else, William Cowper wrote. "Dejection of spirits, which (I suppose) may have prevented many a man from becoming an author, made me one," Cowper penned to his cousin several months after the publication of his second volume of poems, *The Task*. His other hobbies helped, but it was the creative, generative work of writing that absorbed and soothed his mind.[38]

Writing was not a cure-all. Depression's fog so swallowed his mind at times that he could not even do this. His pen would sit idle on the desk, dry of ink. His mind was vacant, incapable of generating words. When it eased enough for him to function, though, he picked up his pen again. This creative act became a salvation, his "best remedy."

He wrote *The Task* through the ebbs and flows of depression. "In the year when I wrote *The Task*, (for it occupied me about a year), I was very often most supremely unhappy," he said, "and am under God indebted in good part to that work for not having been much worse."[39]

Reading Cowper's poetry, I can't help but notice how grounded it is in physical places. This is particularly true of *The Task*. He writes long, lyrical descriptions of his walks in the country. His words transport me to the sacred quiet of the winter woods. When he writes of his garden and his seasonal greenhouse, I smell the damp earth and sweet blossoms.

I have to wonder how much this rootedness played a role in poetry's effectiveness to alleviate his depression. Depression pulled him from reality. It kept his mind jailed in a cycle of morbid thoughts. Nature, however, was tangible, and its beauty was a temporary release from his prison cell. Being outdoors and then recalling its earthy delights as he worked at his writing desk helped pull him from his mind and attend to the physical world.

The release poetry provided was not just from its groundedness, though. The mental exercise, the occupation, the sense of fulfillment in completing something worthwhile—all of these pieces were a remedy in their own right.

Cowper also found solace in translating Homer. The steady work was a refuge:

A thousand times have I been glad of it; for a thousand times it has served at least to divert my attention, in some degree, from such terrible tempests as I believe have seldom been permitted to beat upon a human mind. Let my friends, therefore, who wish me some little measure of tranquillity [*sic*] in the performance of the most turbulent voyage that ever Christian mariner made, be contented, that, having Homer's mountains and forests to windward, I escape, under their shelter, from the force of many a gust that would almost overset me; especially when they consider that, not by choice, but by necessity, I make *them* my refuge.[40]

Sometimes the remedy of poetry came in the form of a good story. One January, caught in another threatening doom, Cowper stopped speaking and responding. His dear friends Mrs. Unwin and Lady Austen tried desperately to pull him from the brink. Around the parlor fire one evening, Lady Austen told him the story of John Gilpin's adventures, embellishing dramatically as she saw him slowly begin to pay attention, saw the sparkle reenter his eye, heard him laugh again. He stayed up all night beginning a poem. Ironically, the poem that emerged, "The Diverting History of John Gilpin," was his most comical one. His delight and sense of accomplishment delayed the onset of his next major crisis.

In spite of his continual depression, Cowper could be quite funny and lighthearted. We see it in the dramatic mishaps of John Gilpin, in his letters, and in brief, occasional poems he wrote for friends. He was an engaging conversationalist, who could delight a table of friends with his stories and "make an amusing story out of *nothing*."[41]

He admits that sometimes this lightheartedness was affected:

If I trifle, and merely trifle, it is because I am reduced to it by necessity—a melancholy that nothing so effectually disperses, engages me sometimes in the arduous task of being merry by force. And, strange as it may seem, the most ludicrous lines I ever wrote have been written in the saddest mood, and but for that saddest mood, perhaps had never been written at all.[42]

Some might look at Cowper's poetry and conclude that while he was writing he couldn't possibly have been depressed. But, with the exception of his deepest crises, poetry was what kept him afloat. It gave him a reason to get up in the morning. It gave him a sense of purpose. It gave a channel to direct his thoughts to. It kept him alive.

I am not a poet, but I understand Cowper's drive to keep moving. Inaction only gave my thoughts a still place to fester. And yet action and effort went against everything depression was doing in me. I wanted to sleep. I wanted to disappear from the world. I knew that if I stopped, though—if I stopped for too long—it would suck me under and I might not get my head above water again. So I kept going to class. I kept reading and studying. I prepared practices for the music ministry I was directing. I met with girls I was mentoring. I went to work. I wrote. I did it in a fog. The effort of it drained me. But I did it. And it kept me alive.

THE CASTAWAY

From the time he moved in with the Unwins shortly after his arrival in Huntingdon, Cowper and Mrs. Unwin were dear friends. He was her companion when she lost her husband suddenly. They moved to Olney together, to Orchard Side, where they lived for nearly twenty years. Then they moved to Weston together, to a sturdy house with gardens and open air. They mourned the early death of her son William together, who was one of Cowper's dearest friends. Mrs. Unwin was his caretaker in each episode of depression and at times the only person he would allow to see him. At least once, she was the one who intervened when he was trying to end his life.

When we read of Cowper and Mary Unwin living together for over thirty years, we can quickly begin to speculate of romance. From the information we have, though, it appears their relationship was entirely proper and platonic. They were briefly engaged to be married, but this seems to have been to preserve appearances regarding a single man and widow living together. The marriage plans were cut short by one of Cowper's major depressive episodes and never picked up again after his recovery several years later. Whether or not there was romance between them, however, it's clear that their love for each other was fierce and deeply devoted.

So when Mrs. Unwin suffered a series of strokes about five years after they'd settled in Weston, and the caretaking roles were reversed, Cowper was disoriented. The person who had been his steadfast friend was unable to walk alone, her words were barely coherent, and her hands, always busy, were still. It was only a matter of time before the emotional weight took its toll. The depression returned full force, including the psychosis he'd experienced earlier in life, and he would not recover before his death.

The word *torture* seems apt to describe Cowper's suffering during these years. The voices and dreams returned, speaking to him of his hopeless state by day and night, and he once again lived under an oppressive terror. A new friend, the Olney school master, Teedon, was the one he turned to for help interpreting these messages. Cowper kept books filled with the voices he heard and Teedon's interpretations of them. The scribblings of his deluded mind slashed the pages of volumes.[43] About this time, he wrote to his friend Hayley, "I am a pitiful beast, and in the texture of my mind and natural temper have three threads of despondency for one of hope."[44]

Under Teedon's advice, Cowper occasionally prayed once again, though he continued to insist he was forbidden to. Even these prayers, though, bear the weight of desperation: "If I endeavour to pray, I get my answer in a double portion of misery. My petitions, therefore, are reduced to three words, and those not very often repeated—'God have mercy!'"[45]

He stopped eating, out of self-inflicted penance. He refused medicine. He took no delight in his friends' company, while also dreading being alone. Even when he finally was awarded a pension from the king, a remarkable affirmation of his literary endeavors, he showed no reaction.

When his cousins discovered the extent of Mrs. Unwin's poor health and Cowper's incapacitation, his young cousin, John Johnson, moved them both to his house, where he cared for Cowper until his death.[46] He took him traveling and twice briefly coaxed him into translating Homer again. In spite of his best attempts, however, nothing alleviated Cowper's depression or quieted the condemning voices haunting his mind. He claimed spirits haunted his bed. Each morning, he stared at Johnson intently, trying to discern if he were actually his cousin or a demon taking his form.[47]

Since Cowper was convinced the voices he heard were real and divine, Johnson tried to counteract them. In a touching expression of love, Johnson secretly installed a series of tubes in the wall beside Cowper's bed, and employed someone whose voice Cowper would not recognize to speak words of hope and comfort through the tubing. It was the only thing he knew to do, a desperate attempt to thwart the voices in Cowper's mind.

While his efforts are moving, it does not appear that Johnson's strategy worked. Cowper continued to deteriorate, continued to dread his end. His thoughts were flimsy, he recorded, like "loose and dry sand, which the closer it is grasped slips the sooner away. Mr. Johnson reads to me, but I lose every other sentence through the inevitable wanderings of my mind."[48] He often said to his dedicated servant, Roberts, at this time, "Wretch that I am to wander thus in chase of false delight."[49]

His letters, frequent and lively earlier in life, nearly ceased for the last five years of his life as depression crippled him to the extent that he could not even write to his dearest friends. The ones he did manage to pen were filled with the bleak words of his depressed mind. They are heartbreaking. He told his cousin, "To wish, therefore, that I had never existed, which has been my only reasonable wish for many years, seems all that remains to one who once dreamed of happiness, but awoke never to dream of it again."[50]

Within a year of his death, Cowper wrote one final poem. He tells the story of a castaway, swept overboard at sea, left behind by his friends who throw things behind their retreating boat in an effort to keep him afloat. As the man slowly succumbs to the waves, Cowper compares himself to him:

> I therefore purpose not, or dream,
>   Descanting on his fate,
> To give the melancholy theme
>   A more enduring date:
> But misery still delights to trace
>   Its semblance in another's case.
>
> No voice divine the storm allay'd,
>   No light propitious shone;
> When, snatch'd from all effectual aid,
>   We perish'd, each alone:
> But I beneath a rougher sea,
>   And whelm'd in deeper gulfs than he.[51]

He was drowning. Drowning alone, pulled down by the weight of despair. He died a year later.

GRACE IN THE VINEGAR BOTTLE

When I close the book on Cowper's earthly life, my heart is heavy. The thought of him walking like a ghost on the earth, lying on his deathbed in "unutterable despair," makes me want to weep. My heart sighs out a little word: *Why?*

Why, God, did he have to suffer so? Why didn't you break in to comfort him with your presence? Why didn't you heal his mind? It's the same question that bubbles up when I see friends today in deep suffering. My heart aches, and my mind struggles to come to terms with why God miraculously heals in some situations—and doesn't in others.

Then I think of Cowper's own words: "God moves in a mysterious way. . . . Judge not the Lord by feeble sense, but trust him for his grace." As I have sat with Cowper's story and with his unresolved pain, I've wondered where this grace came in for him. And again and again, it's come to me—in his friends.

Sometimes Cowper could see the extreme acts of love from his friends. He once told William Unwin, "Every proof of attention and regard to a man who lives in a vinegar bottle is welcome from his friends on the outside of it."[52] But often, he was hardly in touch with reality enough to notice what they did to care for him. We can see the love they poured out on Cowper, though. They make me think of the friends who cared for me during my own dark days. What acts of love did they do that went unseen by my darkened eyes?

For decades, Cowper couldn't see God's mercy for him. He couldn't see his presence. He could only see wrath and despair. But I believe God was still there. He appeared in the people in Cowper's life who steadily and faithfully loved him, even when his depression made him hard to care for. He was in the friends who would not give up hope, even when Cowper felt it had abandoned him, and in the friends who refused to leave him, even when Cowper felt they had left him to drown.

He was there in Mary Unwin, who cared for Cowper year after year, who, even during her own illness, when her own legs were feeble and weak, would ask him to take her for a walk to get him up from the chair where depression had him frozen.

He was there in John Newton, who encouraged Cowper to write and gave him a place in the church, who welcomed him, uninvited, into his home, who kept watch over him to keep him alive.

He was there in his cousin Johnson, who took him into his home, who installed tubing in the walls to whisper words of truth and comfort into Cowper's ears, who strategically left books out for Cowper to find, to keep him writing, to give him a reason to live.

He was there in his friend Hayley, who rushed to his side when he was slowly starving himself and coaxed him to eat, who asked for letters from prominent religious leaders to remind Cowper of the effect his poetry had on the world.

When Cowper died, John Newton said, "What a glorious surprise must it be to find himself released from all his chains in a moment, and in the presence of the Lord whom he loved and whom he served!"[53] What a glorious surprise to close his eyes in despair and then open them and find himself face-to-face with the God who had never left him.

Perhaps you, my friend, are caught in the desolate wilderness of the "not yet." Perhaps you wonder, as Cowper did, whether God has left you. Perhaps you feel you cannot carry on.

Remember that, even in a story as tragic as Cowper's, we can look back and see God's presence. It was in the rescue of his friends and of his art. It was there in a faith that carried on through darkness. It was there in the moments of laughter and delight he shared with friends, with his beloved pets, surrounded by the flowers of his greenhouse. It is in the legacy of the hymns and poems and letters he left behind to encourage us today.

Even if you cannot see it in this moment with your earthly eyes, God is working in your story as well. Follow Cowper's example as one who has walked through this "unfathomable mine" before you. Cling to the people God has brought into your life—and thank them for their care. As much as you are able, embrace the work or activities that will ground you in the present, tangible, earthy bits of life. Keep walking forward in the dark.

5

CHARLES SPURGEON

Cling to the Promises of God

His stomach twisted. So many had come. Thousands stood, pressing in from the garden's entrance to the Music Hall, trying to gain entry to the majestic building. There would be at least another ten thousand inside. So many souls. The weight of it left his hands shaking. He took a deep, steadying breath and followed his guides through the maze of bodies until they reached the pulpit from which he would preach that night.

All seats were occupied, from the floor to the third gallery high above him. Men and women lined the walkways, the stairs, the back wall—any possible standing room—and the room quieted in anticipation. Waiting ten minutes would only allow the crowd to grow restless. They would begin early.

After a Scripture reading, he began to pray, pouring out thanksgiving, pleading for the salvation of those in his hearing. He was caught up, enraptured in the presence of God, this gangly, smooth-cheeked young man borne up to the very Holy of Holies, surrounded by London's masses.

That's when it happened.

He heard a sharp shout. "Fire!" Then another, "The galleries are giving way!" And a third, "The place is falling!" Shrieks and shouts erupted from the reverent silence as hundreds leaped from their seats and rushed for the door, desperate for escape, certain of disaster. It was like water bursting from a dam, raging and violent. With a crash, one of the banisters lining the stairs burst from the pressure of bodies and broke free. It dangled there like a broken wing.

The doorway was a tangled commotion of limbs and bonnets and coattails. Those fleeing from the galleries clawed their way out, and just as quickly, those outside pushed in, eager to take their place inside. It was a pulsing, clamoring mob.

What was happening? His heart beat in his ears as he frantically scanned the room. There was no smoke. There was no sign the building was collapsing.

"It is a false alarm," he bellowed, his arms outstretched in reassurance. "This is the ruse of thieves and pickpockets who would disrupt our worship. Remain calm, my friends."

"Preach!" a man yelled from the crowd. "Yes, preach!" the rest of the crowd chanted.

He paused, unsure. In such confusion, what could he say? The only thing he knew to turn to—the gospel:

"My friends, there is a terrible day coming, when the terror and alarm of this evening shall be as nothing. . . . Many were afraid to stop here, because they thought, if they stayed, they might die, and then they would be damned. . . . But know you not, my friends, that grace, sovereign grace, can yet save you? . . . You are sick and diseased, but Jesus can heal you; and He will if you only trust Him."

A fresh chaos blossomed. More lurched from their seats and ran to the back. The wailing. The screams. Something was terribly wrong. He was suddenly very warm, and a low hum crowded his ears. He could feel himself swaying.

Dead. Crushed. Hospital. The words came to him like on the wind.

"My brain is in a whirl, and I scarcely know where I am, so great are my apprehensions that many persons must have been injured by rushing out. I would rather that you retired gradually, and may

God Almighty dismiss you with His blessing, and carry you in safety. . . ."

His lips moved to form the words, but he could hardly hear himself, so great was the roaring. He could see bodies now, circled by onlookers, limbs twisted at unnatural angles. Darkness pressed in from the corner of his vision. "Do not be in a hurry. Let those nearest the door go first," he managed. Then the world went dark.[1]

DUNGEONS OF DESPAIR: SLANDER AND CATASTROPHE

When Spurgeon's deacons carried him, only partially conscious, through a private exit that night, he was only twenty-two years old. He didn't see the seven bloodied corpses on the grass in front of the Surrey Gardens Music Hall or the other twenty-eight people carried to the hospital badly injured. He only heard later the account of those who had maliciously sounded a false alarm, of those who had fallen in the rush and been trampled underfoot.

Can you imagine the grief in the city that night? Can you imagine the realization that those people had come to hear you preach—that the attack had happened on your watch?

Spurgeon's critics did not spare him in the aftermath of the tragedy. They heaped slander and accusation on his sorrow, blaming him for the lives lost and injured. But this was not the first time he'd come under their harsh words.

Charles Spurgeon had come to London three years earlier, a fresh-faced, nineteen-year-old country boy with a bad haircut. In spite of his rustic manners and no formal theological training, he was a dynamic and dramatic preacher, passionate about the Word of God. Within two years, the two-hundred-member congregation of New Park Street Chapel exploded in size to the point that their building could not contain them. He would remain their pastor for nearly forty years.

He was not popular with everyone, though. He faced harsh criticism and slander in the papers. They misquoted him and attributed

words to him he'd never uttered. Some doubted his salvation. Others
compared his words "that are smoother than butter" to the deception
of Satan.[2] One critic called his sermons a "prostitution of the pulpit."[3]
I have trouble discerning if these critics were jealous of his popularity,
turned off by his unique style (which they called "bad taste" and
"vulgar and theatrical"), or giving their genuine estimation.[4]

It is clear that these attacks hurt Spurgeon keenly. When he was
trying to preach the gospel and win souls for Christ, such blatant
attacks on his character were agonizing. I can't help but remember
that he was a tender young man, far from home and just learning his
way in the world.

During these early years, when his new wife, Susannah, was trying
to find a way to comfort him, she carefully printed Matthew 5:11-12
and hung it up in their bedroom. Every morning, as he dressed and
walked from the room to begin his day, and every night, as he rested
after another day of work, it greeted him: "Blessed are ye, when men
shall revile you, and persecute you, and shall say all manner of evil
against you falsely, for my sake. Rejoice, and be exceeding glad: for
great is your reward in heaven: for so persecuted they the prophets
which were before you" (KJV).

In spite of the slander, Spurgeon now had a congregation in need
of a space to hold their growing numbers. They began construction
on a new, five-thousand-seat church, the Metropolitan Tabernacle,
and while they waited, they rented spaces to hold the swelling
crowds flocking to hear their sensational preacher. This was what
took them to Surrey Gardens Music Hall.

After Spurgeon was carried from the Hall on that tragic night,
"more dead than alive," he was taken away to a friend's home for
seclusion and quiet. In the moments of chaos in the Hall, anxiety
overwhelmed him to the point of losing consciousness. Though he'd
watched the confusion and injuries from afar, the experience was
traumatic for him, and I believe he felt he was in some way responsible for the loss of life. In the days that followed, guilt and sorrow

over the whole affair plunged him into depression. Susannah and his concerned deacons watched his anguish, shielding him from the worst of the slander being heaped on him by the press. Any word about the tragedy, or even the sight of the Bible, was enough to bring him to tears.

He later described what this season was like for him:

> Who can conceive the anguish of my sad spirit? I refused to be comforted; tears were my meat by day, and dreams my terror by night. I felt as I had never felt before. 'My thoughts were all a case of knives,' cutting my heart in pieces, until a kind of stupor of grief ministered a mournful medicine to me. . . . Here my mind lay, like a wreck upon the sand, incapable of its usual motion. I was in a strange land, and a stranger in it. My Bible, once my daily food, was but a hand to lift the sluices of my woe. Prayer yielded no balm to me. . . . 'Broken in pieces all asunder,' my thoughts, which had been to me a cup of delights, were like broken glass, the piercing and cutting miseries of my pilgrimage.[5]

Do his words sound like a page torn from a tear-stained journal (albeit polished with a bit of refined Victorian English)? If you have ever been locked in the hell-like "dungeons underneath the Castle of Despair," perhaps you recognize these cries from the dark.[6] Day and night he could not escape his haunting thoughts, even while he tried to turn his thoughts to Jesus and the love of God. He couldn't think straight. He couldn't pray. He couldn't find comfort. His depression was so severe that the deacons wondered if he'd ever be able to preach again. Susannah feared he would lose his reason entirely.

One day, though, when walking with Susannah in the garden, Spurgeon stopped suddenly. She saw in his eyes an old brightness when he began to speak: "Dearest, how foolish I have been! Why! what does it matter what becomes of me, if the Lord shall but be glorified? If Christ be exalted, let Him do as He pleases with me."[7]

In that moment, the words of Philippians 2:9-11 had struck him with a burst of light and comfort: "Wherefore God also hath highly exalted him, and given him a name which is above every name: That at the name of Jesus every knee should bow, of things in heaven, and things in earth, and things under the earth; And that every tongue should confess that Jesus Christ is Lord, to the glory of God the Father" (KJV).

Here was a promise Spurgeon could cling to. Though he stood in a world where evil and tragedy prospered, though he stood in darkness, Christ's kingdom was still safe, his throne still unshakable.[8] It was enough to pull Spurgeon back from the brink of a complete mental breakdown. It was enough to bring back the song of hope to his heart, though he was still unable to speak of what had happened.

Spurgeon did not, with this one spiritual revelation, throw off his depression and instantly recover. He would carry the memories and effects of the tragedy with him for the rest of his life.[9] Even twenty-five years later, a similar situation of confusion in an overcrowded hall completely disarmed him.[10] I can imagine him slumped against the wall, his forehead wedging his wrist against the plaster, resisting the memories, breathing deeply to still his heart and fight back the horror rising in his throat.

WHEN THE BODY CONQUERS YOUR SOUL

Though the sorrow of the Surrey Hall disaster would never be erased, Spurgeon eventually found glimmers of God's redemptive goodness brought from it.

The ministry at the Metropolitan Tabernacle was prospering. Hundreds and thousands were coming to Christ. His sermons were printed weekly and read around the world, and his critics eventually accepted his presence, even while there were some people who would never approve of his preaching. He'd founded the Pastor's College for the training of a new generation of preachers and started a magazine, *The Sword and the Trowel*.

He was married to a woman he loved, a woman who made him an even more effective minister through her support. They were watching their twin sons grow into strong young men.

The level of success could have been nearly intoxicating. But about this time, Spurgeon's body began to turn against him. By his thirty-fifth birthday, he had experienced the first pains of gout, a severe and extremely painful form of rheumatoid arthritis. He endured its "baptism of pain" episodically for the rest of his life.[11]

Gout was cruel in its misery. One day Spurgeon would be in good health, cheerful, abuzz with productivity, and the next, with little warning, the pain would come. It seeped into his bones, piercing, throbbing, causing a shuddering that made him feel as if he would break apart with agony. Painful and swollen joints made it impossible to use his hands to write or even to dress himself. It was a "mercy" to be able to roll over in bed—or to have only one joint torturing him at a time.

The pain left him exhausted, unable to sleep for its intensity, his body tense in the fighting of it. It also clouded his mind, sending a fog over his thoughts. He was caught in the no-man's land between death and the agony of not dying. Anyone who has suffered from extreme physical pain will recognize the echoes of this anguish.

Some people with chronic illnesses are undoubtedly able to still live with a joy that defies human reason. A physical ailment—even if it's particularly painful—does not automatically mean that you will become depressed. But certain sicknesses—or the inclination of a person—allow the disease to "touch not only the bone and the flesh, but also the mind. The pain of the mind encroaches upon the spirit and the spirit is darkened with trouble."[12] This was Spurgeon's experience.

When these episodes laid him low, it was unthinkable for him to preach or attend to his normal duties. All he could muster from his sickbed were letters to his beloved congregation. Once, after being away from church for twelve weeks, he wrote the following words to them, mingling "the groans of pain and the songs of hope": "The furnace still glows around me. . . . I have been brought very low; my flesh has been tortured with pain, and my spirit has been prostrate with depression. . . . I am as a potter's vessel when it is utterly broken, useless, and laid aside. Nights of watching, and days of weeping have been mine."[13]

Even as he recovered, Spurgeon couldn't help but remember that he was not the only one who suffered. There was one "near to his heart" who remained in pain: his wife, Susannah. After they'd had several precious years together, an unknown disease wracked her body with "constant, wearying pain," leaving her a semi-invalid.[14]

Our poor friend Spurgeon. His body was breaking. Depression came in waves. He bore the weight of ministering to thousands. Then, on top of it all, he had to watch his beloved wife endure a pain he could not remove or remedy—and sometimes he had to do this even from afar, as he traveled for preaching engagements and his own seasons of convalescence.

As the years wore on and his condition worsened, Spurgeon was forced to leave London occasionally for a climate more conducive to healing from his arthritic symptoms. He frequented Menton, on the coast of France. It would be during one such trip that he would die. It was the only trip on which Susannah was well enough to travel with him.

THE GOSPEL BETRAYED: THE DOWNGRADE CONTROVERSY

Five years before that final trip to the temperate Mediterranean coast, Spurgeon became embroiled in controversy over a new theology making its inroads into his Baptist denomination. He grew concerned as he saw the authority of Scripture being questioned along with basic gospel tenets like the sinfulness of humanity, the divinity of Christ, and the necessity of Jesus' substitutionary atonement on the cross.

Believing the denomination was on a downgrade, sliding ever further from the truth of the whole gospel, Spurgeon published a series of articles in *The Sword and the Trowel*, calling for a renewed commitment to orthodoxy within the Baptist Union. The articles received harsh backlash, and he eventually withdrew from the denomination. Its members, in the name of maintaining peace and unity, closed the internal discussions he'd hoped to start with a vote of censure on his comments. His own brother voted in favor of the motion. He was devastated.

Though he did not like conflict or controversy, Spurgeon saw the entire episode as a valiant and necessary fight for truth and a defense of the gospel he held so dear.[15] And yet, with his conviction came heartache. Relationships splintered as he was deserted by friends, colleagues, students, and ministry partners. He lost significant financial support. The pangs of betrayal struck his heart. Susannah called this season "the deepest grief of his noble life."[16]

In a letter to a friend during this time, he wrote, "I entreat your prayers, for I am heart-sore and weary with the desertions of those who should be at my side. . . . I am a poor creature for so great a battle. HE [*sic*] covereth my head, and yet I am ready to die."[17]

The controversy put a strain on his already poor health. Though the height of it lasted only two years, for the final five years of Spurgeon's life, there was hardly a month in which his *Sword and Trowel* publication didn't have an article addressing it.[18] The effect on him was so severe that some called him a martyr for the truth.[19]

WHEN SAINTS HAVE NO JOY

If these stories were the full picture of Spurgeon's depression, we could easily believe it was entirely circumstantial. The trying times he faced would bludgeon anyone's emotions, and he was left like a child in the dark.

But depression for Spurgeon was more than just circumstantial. When he spoke of it in his sermons and lectures, his examples, which were often rooted in his own experience, included a significant form of depression: the kind that comes without cause. In one sermon, he said,

You may be surrounded with all the comforts of life and yet be in wretchedness more gloomy than death if the spirits are depressed. You may have no outward cause whatever for sorrow and yet if the mind is dejected, the brightest sunshine will not relieve your gloom. . . . There are times when all our evidences get clouded and all our joys are fled. Though we may still cling to the Cross, yet it is with a desperate grasp.[20]

Spurgeon understood that depression isn't always logical, and its cause is not always clear. There are times, he said, when our spirits betray us, and we sink into darkness. We slip into the "bottomless pits" where our souls "can bleed in ten thousand ways, and die over and over again each hour."[21] There is no reasoning, and a remedy is hard to find.

As well fight with the mist as with this shapeless, undefinable, yet, all-beclouding hopelessness. One affords himself no pity when in this case, because it seems to be unreasonable, and even sinful to be troubled without manifest cause; and yet troubled the man is, even in the very depths of his spirit . . . [it] needs a heavenly hand to push it back . . . but nothing short of this will chase away the nightmare of the soul.[22]

I am so thankful for quotes like this from Spurgeon because you can hear his understanding. I remember how helpless I felt in my depression, how it seemed I was powerless to do anything to escape from it. Some people expected there to be a quick fix, a logical solution, or some sort of spiritual willpower that could defeat it, but light and joy were evasive.

Spurgeon clearly knew this helplessness *and* how poorly people can react to it. He spoke directly to harsh and insensitive "helpers" from the pulpit—those who were quick to cast blame, quick to tell depressed people to just pull themselves out of it, and slow to show compassion.[23] He also would not tolerate the accusation that "good

Christians" do not get depressed. "God's people sometimes walk in darkness, and see no light. There are times when the best and brightest of saints have no joy," he preached.[24] He was clear that not only was depression not a guaranteed sign of whether or not someone was a Christian; it also wasn't a sign of whether or not they were growing in their faith. It was possible to be faithful and depressed: "Depression of spirit is no index of declining Grace—the very loss of joy and the absence of assurance may be accompanied by the greatest advancement in the spiritual life."[25] Oh for more pastors to preach this way on depression!

MAKE GOOD USE OF YOUR AFFLICTION

Perhaps you know the feeling of your spirits being so low that you can do nothing, contribute nothing. You are overwhelmed and paralyzed by sadness. Your brain is foggy, your temper sharp. All is dark. Then the questions come: *What if this endures? What if I can never do anything of lasting value again?*

Spurgeon knew this feeling. Perhaps this is why, in a lecture to his students on depression, he told them, "Think not that all is over with your usefulness."[26] He was laid low many times both physically and emotionally, but it didn't stop his ministry. He wrote thousands of sermons and countless letters, read prolifically, met with people, prayed with people, organized ministries, taught at the Pastor's College. His suffering did not exclude him from usefulness. If anything, the fruit of it made him *more* useful. His experience with depression enabled him to encourage and support others who suffered from it as well.

For example, Spurgeon warned his students to be aware of situations in which they may be more susceptible to depression. The list he gave them runs like an autobiographical catalog:

- when you have prolonged illness or physical problems
- when you do intense mental or "heart" work

- when you're lonely or isolated
- when your lifestyle is sedentary and you overwork your brain
- after success
- before success
- after one heavy blow
- through the slow pile of trouble and discouragement
- in exhaustion and overworking

Or it could simply come without cause, without reason, without justification, which he considered to be the most painful of all.[27]

Spurgeon offered compassionate and practical advice to his parishioners as well, preaching to them about such things as the need for rest: "The spirit needs to be fed and the body needs feeding also. Do not forget these matters! It may seem to some people that I ought not to mention such small things as food and rest, but these may be the very first elements in really helping a poor depressed servant of God."[28] Self-care is not merely a modern notion. Spurgeon understood from his own experience that taking proper care of our bodies is an important part of fighting depression, and he freely shared his hard-earned wisdom.

Because of his own suffering, he could also better sympathize with and comfort others. People would come from miles around to seek his advice and consolation, and those who couldn't come physically would write letters. He was a "wounded healer"—someone who used his own sorrow to bring others comfort:

> It is a great gift to have learned by experience how to sympathize. "Ah!" I say to them, "I have been where you are!" They look at me and their eyes say, "No, surely you never felt as we do." I therefore go further, and say, "If you feel worse than I did, I pity you, indeed, for I could say with Job, 'My soul chooses strangling rather than life.' I could readily enough have laid violent hands upon myself to escape from my misery of spirit."[29]

There is a profound comfort in realizing someone else understands—at least in part—your suffering. They can offer comfort in a way others cannot. This is part of the power of the stories in this book—to find others who understand, who can say, "I have been where you are." Surviving painful experiences like depression puts us in a unique position and bestows on us a unique responsibility to offer this comfort and camaraderie to others. Spurgeon encourages us not to forget this: "He who has been in the dark dungeon knows the way to the bread and the water. If you have passed through depression, and the Lord has appeared to your comfort, lay yourself out to help others who are where you used to be."[30]

Your usefulness is not over, Spurgeon tells us. You, too, can be a companion to one in the dark.

SING IN THE DARKNESS

When I think of the word Spurgeon speaks to us from the inheritance of his own struggles, it brings to mind a boisterous hymn I remember singing in my childhood church.

> Standing on the promises that cannot fail,
> When the howling storms of doubt and fear assail,
> By the living Word of God I shall prevail,
> *Standing on the promises of God.*

In the lowest points of Spurgeon's life, it was the promises of God in Scripture that lifted him from despair.

In the early years, when he was depressed and distraught over the harsh criticism flung at him, he looked at the verse in Susannah's script: "Blessed are ye when men shall revile you. . . ."

As the years went by, another verse replaced it, again in his wife's hand: "I have chosen thee in the furnace of affliction" (Isaiah 48:10 KJV).

After the Surrey Gardens Music Hall disaster, a revelation from Scripture encouraged him and pulled him from collapse.

And repeatedly in his sermons, the words of Scripture and the lives of biblical characters encouraged him. They reminded him of truth. They kept him singing. They kept him alive. It was here, where the promises of God collided with his own sorrow, that he found hope.

In the introduction of the *Cheque Book of Faith*, which he wrote in the midst of the Downgrade Controversy, Spurgeon says this: "I believe all the promises of God, but many of them I have personally tried and proved.... I would say to [fellow Christians] in their trials— My brethren, God is good. He will not forsake you: He will bear you through.... Everything else will fail, but His word never will."[31]

Do you hear him speaking to you, my friend? *Trust him. Rest in his promises. Hold on to hope.*

"Ah, yes, Spurgeon," we might say, "but this is so difficult." He knew this. He felt this struggle, the struggle for belief, for faith, the struggle to hold on to the hope of the promises. He knew the temptations of doubt. He knew how depression made them even more difficult to withstand, how much easier it was to question God's goodness, his faithfulness, his abiding presence: "That perpetual assaulting, that perpetual stabbing, and cutting, and hacking at one's faith, is not so easy to endure."[32] But endure we must. And it is precisely "by enduring that we learn to endure."[33] Our trials make these promises richer and make our faith in them even stronger as we see again and again that they are robust enough to sustain us. They teach us humble dependence on a faithful God.

Spurgeon was not saying that the solution to suffering and depression lies in the mantra many depressed Christians have had to endure: just read the Bible, just pray more, just have faith. There is no depression cure-all, no quick spiritual fix. But when we are in the darkness, the promises of Scripture are strong enough to keep us tethered. Knowing that we belong to Christ is an anchor. When we are flailing about, when we don't know if we can go on, when we feel lost, when the darkness consumes us, we cling to God's promises, even when we hardly have the strength to believe them. They are sure, regardless of our feelings, regardless of our outward state.

When we see people from the Bible like Elijah, who wanted to die, and the psalmists, who wrestled with depression and feelings of abandonment by God, and "we find ourselves in similar places," Spurgeon preached, "we are relieved by discovering that we are walking along a path which others have traversed before us."[34] We see these saints cast into darkness. We see God's faithfulness. We see his promises that are strong enough to hold them—and us as well. Don't be dismayed, their stories remind us. This is a trial many have had to endure. You are still his. The Christ who bought you will not abandon you in the dark.

Spurgeon once said, "In the night of sorrow ... believers [are] like nightingales, and they sing in the darkness. There is no real night to a man of a nightingale spirit."[35] It reminds me of a note I received once from a friend: "You are brave. You stand in the darkness, whispering Truth back to yourself." I felt anything but brave at the time. It had been a hard year. It had been a year of tears and questions and fitful nights. And here was my closest friend calling me brave. I couldn't believe it. I wasn't brave—I was desperate. What else could I do in that dark place but keep whispering Truth? It was all I could do to keep the darkness at bay, to keep it from suffocating me.

This is what Spurgeon offers to us. A reminder to sing God's promises. Sing of his faithfulness. Even if you can't see it yet, even if you don't feel it—whisper the Truth to yourself. Sing in the darkness.

6

MOTHER TERESA

Follow Jesus, Not Your Feelings

M uggy air carried the cacophony of the streets through the windows of the bare chapel. Even in this place of quiet prayer, Calcutta begged for their love. The rumble of engines and tinny bleep of car horns reminded them of their calling. They met Jesus not only on their knees but in the form of the poor—the emaciated bodies of street children, the dying covered with sores, the sick with no one to care for them.

Today, the sounds eased the suffocating silence in her heart.

Oh, Absent One, how long will You stay away? I long for You, but You do not want me. Emptiness. Pain. Loneliness. I cannot express this pain. This is what hell is like—without God—no love, no faith. The pain is so great I feel as if everything will break. Who am I that You would forsake me?

She looked at the sisters bent in prayer. They knelt with her in rows on mats covering the floor, their heads draped with the simple white and blue saris of their order. If only they knew of the pain in her heart. They thought her life with Jesus to be filled with consolation, rich with communion—but there were more thorns than roses in that garden. She told them of his love. She guided them in their devotion to him. But her heart was empty. She taught them of his closeness even while she asked in her heart, "Where is Jesus?" There was no God within her. Yet she hid her misery with a cloak of cheerfulness.

Do not let my soul be deceived. Do not let me *deceive anyone. Please God, do not let me spoil the Work. The Work is Yours.*

It was the one surety she had—the work was his. These sisters were his. They were living sacrifices of love, caring for Jesus in the distressing disguise of the poor. She had seen him gather the sisters—and then the brothers—for his service. The world took notice and bestowed gifts and awards. But all she wanted was him. Why did he give all these other things but not himself? Why did he leave her alone to walk in the dark?

Father, may I take what You give and give what You take. Let me not refuse You. So close I come to saying "No." Grant me courage to keep smiling at You, to smile at the Hand that strikes me, to smile at the Hand nailing me to the cross. All I can do, is like a little dog follow in Your—my Master's—footsteps. Sweet Jesus, let me be a cheerful dog. Give me the strength to keep saying "Yes," to smile at Your Hidden Face—always.[1]

The Great "Contradiction"

The world knows her name. Mother Teresa.[2] The saint of Calcutta.

From the days of her youth in what is now North Macedonia, she longed to "love God as He had never been loved before." She pledged her life to his service as a nun with the Sisters of Loreto. The religious congregation's commitment to education took her to India to teach. There this spunky young woman excelled. For nearly twenty years, she cared for her students and, eventually, as principal, the teachers under her care. Her sisters looked on and perceived her precious and intimate relationship with Jesus.

In this season of sweetness and light, she received a call (apparently in the form of a series of visions and voices) to form a new congregation—the Missionaries of Charity. Jesus called her to be his light in the "dark holes" of the poorest of the poor in Calcutta, to become his hands and feet in serving the impoverished and destitute.

After waiting nearly two years for her spiritual superiors' approval, Mother Teresa bravely parted ways with her order to found her new congregation. The beginnings of the Missionaries of Charity were far from glamorous. She walked away from all she knew, all comforts, all security. She had no home, no followers, and only five rupees in her pocket. She went in blind obedience with, as she herself put it, "very little courage."[3]

As the years passed, though, God blessed her ministry, and the Missionaries of Charity grew. Sisters were added to the order. They founded homes for the dying and destitute and programs for street children. They went to the slums and cared for the sick. Once church authorities granted approval to begin foundations outside of Calcutta, the Missionaries of Charity slowly spread throughout the world, in every place caring for those who were unwanted, uncared for, and forgotten.[4] As their foundress, Mother Teresa received international acclaim, eventually including the Nobel Peace Prize, for her undying love for "the least of these."

But under the surface, behind the wrinkled smile that graced the suffering, was a woman who herself was suffering. From the time she first obeyed God's call to begin her life as a Missionary of Charity, the intimacy she enjoyed with him disappeared. It was as if, when she stepped out in her greatest dependence on him, he became silent. She no longer felt his presence. She felt alone, abandoned. "The Work" flourished, but she was desolate.

It is startling to read Mother Teresa's words to her spiritual advisers about this struggle. She is held up as someone particularly close to God—a saint. She is remembered as one full of love and joy. And yet in the deepest places of her heart, she had none of the feelings we would expect. The following letter to her confessor gives a vivid picture of the state of her heart, mind, and soul "in the darkness":

> Lord, my God, who am I that You should forsake me? The child of Your love—and now become as the most hated one— the one You have thrown away as unwanted—unloved. I call, I cling, I want—and there is no One to answer—no One on Whom I can cling—no, No One.—Alone. The darkness is so dark—and I am alone.—Unwanted, forsaken.—The loneliness of the heart that wants love is unbearable.—Where is my faith?—even deep down, right in, there is nothing but emptiness & darkness.—My God—how painful is this unknown pain. It pains without ceasing.—I have no faith.—I dare not utter the words & thoughts that crowd in my heart—& make me suffer untold agony. So many unanswered questions live within me—I am afraid to uncover them—because of the blasphemy.—If there be God,—please forgive me.—Trust that all will end in Heaven with Jesus.—When I try to raise my thoughts to Heaven—there is such convicting emptiness that those very thoughts return like sharp knives & hurt my very soul.—Love—the word—it brings nothing.—I am told God loves me—and yet the reality of darkness & coldness & emptiness is so great that nothing touches my soul.[5]

Emotion gave way to numbness. The fullness of God's presence morphed into a vacant shell. She cried out to the heavens, "Do you see me here? Why have you forsaken me?" But then she wondered if there was even anyone to hear her call. If only God would give her a little comfort, a little sign of his tender care. If only she had the strength to hold on to faith. The pain ran deep, too deep to hold on to certainty. She fumbled in the dark, hoping she would not lose her way. With the exception of one month of respite, she remained in this dark night of faith for nearly fifty years, all the way until her death. Hers was a journey of faith, not sight.

A Heart of Stone: Was Mother Teresa Depressed?

For decades, few knew of Mother Teresa's internal turmoil. The "cloak" of her smile hid her anguish even from those closest to her. Only after her death did the world discover her pain.[6] Since then, some have used the revelation of her spiritual suffering to try to discredit her. They've analyzed her motives and made judgments of her psyche. They've declared her a fraud, a charlatan who paraded a mask of faith to cover her doubt and despair. Her harshest critics have even used her experience to slander the God she worshiped and the faith she devoted her life to. But her own words tell us a different story. Mother Teresa's smile was not disingenuous or hypocritical. It was a response of faith in Jesus and love for him, an attempt to joyfully accept whatever he gave or withheld from her, even if it was his presence. She made a vow during her days in Loreto to not refuse Jesus anything. Her smile was her constant means of saying yes to Jesus, even when it hid a broken heart. We cannot deny that the testament of her life is filled with self-giving labors and iconic joy.

But must we, as she says, accept everything—even the deepest pain—with a smile? As much as I admire Mother Teresa, I can't bring myself to agree with her about this. I believe there is space in the Christian life for mourning, for lament, and, yes, even for doubt. In the Garden of Gethsemane, faithful submission to God's will led to Jesus himself being stretched out on the ground, weeping, in agony. And in my own life, sometimes faith and joy abide while tears stream down my face.

As I look at Mother Teresa's outward legacy, I wonder what to do with the darkness she describes. Was she depressed? I cannot definitively answer that question. It's possible. But the letters to her confessors and closest spiritual advisers are the only evidence we have of her struggles, and though they do reveal her spiritual state, they do not provide enough information for us to gauge whether or not she suffered from clinical depression.

What I do know is that, as I read her words—her prayers, her questions, her doubts—I hear refrains of my own cries from the dark. I see something I recognize. So whether or not Mother Teresa was actually depressed, her presence is still required in the pages of this book. We cannot diagnose her psychological state, but many of us find in her a fellow sojourner, with spiritual trials akin to what we have experienced in depression. She speaks to us wisdom of how to navigate the spiritual life when heaven seems to have gone silent, when prayers echo into the void, when the consolations of faith disappear. She offers an example of how to continue in the spiritual life when we feel we are simply groping in the dark.

Depression often affects our sense of the spiritual life. I know I am not alone in the experience of feeling abandoned by God in my deepest need. The sharpest pain, the thickest darkness, and I sit with the silence of God. No emotion. No certainty. Prayers are a struggle. Scripture loses its sweetness. I wonder what the point of it all is. Is it worth the pain? Why would he leave me here when I need him most? I am the disciples tossed about on the waves while he is sleeping. I am Mary and Martha wrapping the lifeless body of their brother, laying him in a tomb, sealing him from sight—and Jesus is not there. My soul aches with the question of the psalmist, the cry of Christ on the cross: *My God, my God, why have you forsaken me?*

In a time when our bodies are exhausted, our minds befuddled, our hearts laden with grief, the thought of one more area of effort, of failure, of futility is nearly more than we can bear. Some of us are tempted to abandon faith. We can be at a loss about how to pursue it as the ground shifts. So much of this is based on the perception of our feelings. I don't feel God's presence, so I think myself abandoned or wonder if he cares. My heart balks at the words of Scripture because they don't bring tangible comfort—so I question if they are true. My faith doesn't "feel" the same or depression incapacitates my ability to engage with it as I once did, so I question its genuineness.

This is where Mother Teresa's example offers us a way forward. She reminds us that faith and our faithfulness are bigger than our feelings. The emotions and comforts and "warm fuzzies" of faith are wonderful when they come, but they are not the litmus test of God's existence, the gospel's hope, or the faith he planted in my soul. These realities are bigger than the feelings that become clouded and deadened by depression.

Mother Teresa also reminds us that our feelings are not the true test of our growth in holiness. We can continue to be shaped as followers of Jesus, to have his fruit cultivated in our souls. Fruits of love, kindness, humility, and even joy can grow in the dark. We may not see them—or rather, "feel" them—but that does not mean they are not there. Depression does not halt our growth in godliness. It does not put our spiritual life on pause. Mother Teresa shows us what this looks like lived out.

She once said, "Thank God we have been told to follow Christ.—As I have not to go ahead of Him, even in darkness the path is sure. When some days are above the average—I just stand like a very small child and wait patiently for the storm to subside."[7] The lights went out. The path ahead became unclear. But she kept walking. She went forward, not dependent on feelings, and in spite of the doubts the lack of them stirred in her soul. She did not allow those feelings to make her give up on faith, even when it felt that her faith had dissolved. She trained her eyes on the faintest outline of Jesus her Savior—and she kept walking. She followed Jesus in the dark.

Mother Teresa's faith might seem too herculean for us to attain. But let me assure you, there were times when her belief felt weak. She questioned God's existence and doubted her own faith. Words intended for spiritual comfort brought only more questions.

We see this in some of the counsel given to her by her spiritual advisors, such as when one of them reminded her of God's closeness. This is told to many who question God's presence in the midst of pain. I've heard it. I've said it to other people—because I believe it's true. Scripture shows us a God who is close to the brokenhearted, who draws near to the weak, who enters into the mess with us. But it can be hard for this truth to resonate in our depressed, broken hearts. Mother Teresa wrote, "My soul is just like [an] ice block—I have nothing to say.—You say He is 'so close that you can neither see nor hear Him, not even taste His presence.' I don't understand this, Father—and yet I wish I could understand it."[8] She did not understand how God could be close when her heart felt as it did, but she wanted to understand. She continued to move forward in faith that somehow, somewhere, in some form, he was still there. Seeing her wrestling with her faith in ways I recognize brings a strange sort of comfort. It gives me permission to struggle as well and to know that struggling does not have to undermine my walk with God.

HELPLESS BUT DARING: PRAYER AND OBEDIENCE IN THE DARK

Regardless of her feelings, Mother Teresa continued to turn to Jesus in prayer. But prayer (and other spiritual disciplines as well) looked different in the dark than they had in seasons of light and warmth and delight. They felt different. The "help & consolation" they used to provide was gone.[9] Instead, her heart was filled with pain and longing.

> Sometimes—I just hear my own heart cry out—"My God" and nothing else comes.—The torture and pain I can't explain. . . . Before I could spend hours before Our Lord—loving Him—talking to Him—and now—not even meditation goes properly—nothing but "My God"—even that sometimes does not come.—Yet deep down somewhere in my heart that longing for God keeps breaking through the darkness.[10]

The oneness she had experienced with God in prayer and the sense of being in his presence dissipated to the extent that she insisted she did not pray, could not pray any longer. Her lips shaped words, but they no longer brought a sense of connection or peace. She wrestled with God's very existence, but still she directed all of these thoughts and feelings to him—still she prayed.

She prayed, and Jesus met her on the way. He met her in her stifled words. He met her as she was surrounded by the prayers of her sisters during their community prayers. He met her as she walked the streets of Calcutta. She prayed boldly of her pain, even telling God she didn't know if she believed in him: "Darkness is such that I really do not see—neither with my mind nor with my reason.—The place of God in my soul is blank."[11] Regardless of her feelings, she brought her thoughts, her questions, and her hurt before God.

In this sense, her letters and prayers remind me of the lament psalms in the Bible. She didn't know what to pray and sometimes wasn't convinced that God was listening or that he was even there. But she turned her aching heart to him, kept praying, kept calling out. She pounded on heaven's door, begging God to listen, begging him to appear. This did not remove her pain. It did not bring instant light to her darkness. But it did keep her in the right place—at his feet. And that small, simple, childlike faith and dependence was enough to keep her going for a lifetime.

Another practice that helped Mother Teresa find her way in the dark was obedience. She once called it "the only thing that keeps me on the surface."[12] She had once heard God's call. She had been called to dedicate her life to his service, to follow him in serving the poor, to lead a religious congregation, to care for him by meeting the needs of the suffering. So, even when her interior life became "icy cold," even when all within was "darkness," she carried on in "blind faith."[13] In one letter, she wrote,

> If there is hell—this must be one. How terrible it is to be without God—no prayer—no faith—no love.—The only thing that still remains—is the conviction that the work is His—that the Sisters & the Brothers are His.—And I cling to this as the

person having nothing clings to the straw—before drowning.— And yet, Father—in spite of all these—I want to be faithful to Him—to spend myself for Him, to love Him not for what He gives but for what He takes—to be at His disposal.[14]

She did not understand everything. She did not have answers to why she suffered. But she continued to follow her last marching orders, taking steps each day in obedience the best way she knew how. The knowledge that she was doing God's work was reassuring when all else felt lost.

Mother Teresa's attitude is inspiring, but I'm left wondering how I'm to emulate it. Our situations are so different. I'm not a nun, bound to obedience to my religious superiors. I do not have a clear, specific call as she did.

I also know how debilitating depression can be. Like any illness, it affects each of us differently. Like any illness, it forces some of us to "walk with a limp" and leaves others flat on their backs. Some of us may be able to continue in our jobs or keep muddling through our activities and responsibilities. Others of us can barely get out of bed each day.

Depression does not show some of us to be more obedient or faithful than others. I do not want to use Mother Teresa's example to say that we must will our way to wholeness or that those of us incapacitated by depression are weak, disobedient, or faithless.

But I think Mother Teresa still has something to teach us here. We, too, can seek to be faithful and obedient in the midst of our deep pain. This does not need to be a grandiose act—and it does not need to lead to guilt over all the things depression keeps us from doing. (We have enough guilt already.) It may be as simple as getting out of bed, choosing life by putting our feet on the floor. It may be taking our medication as prescribed by our doctors or taking the brave step of asking for help. It may be exercising or letting that friend take you for coffee. It is taking the next little step already at your feet.

God has prepared "good works . . . in advance for us to do" (Ephesians 2:10 NIV). He has created you with unique passions and skills, with a beautiful way only you can image him to the world. He has invited you to participate in the work of his kingdom. "Obedience" to this "call" is living each moment in faith that you still believe this to be true, even when your world and your vision of that kingdom are dim. Follow Jesus there, in those tiny, faltering ways. This is what it means to be faithful.

LEARNING LOVE IN SUFFERING

As Mother Teresa sought to follow Jesus faithfully, her pain carved out deep places within her to care for others. She looked for Jesus in the dark—and she found him in the darkness experienced by other people. She found his presence in suffering.

She spoke often of caring for those who were unwanted and uncared for—this was the worst form of poverty, she insisted. Her empathy for them only grew as she went year by year feeling unwanted, uncared for, abandoned, and neglected by God herself. She said, "The physical situation of my poor left in the streets unwanted, unloved, unclaimed—are the true picture of my own spiritual life, of my love for Jesus."[15] She knew the pain they experienced—and the pain she endured fostered greater empathy. Suffering birthed love. This is how she would later come to say, "I have come to love the darkness"[16]—because she found it to be part of the work, part of her ability to minister to others.

I am not suggesting we need to come to "love the darkness" of depression any more than I would come to love a broken leg. Pain is pain, and there is no need for spiritualized masochism. But any form of pain, including depression, can shape us in positive ways if we let it. God can, in his grace, transform the effects of our pain into something good. The resurrecting God, who brings life out of dead things, can take the ashes of our agony and create beauty. He can use our suffering to teach us to love.

This is also not where I tell you that you'll be able to sense this process as it occurs. No, most of the time we keep company with the questions and the aching. We ask, as Mother Teresa did, "Where is Jesus? How long will he stay away?" We wonder how God could use us. We are so utterly stripped of thought and emotion that the possibility of such a hope doesn't register.

But then one day you sit across the table from someone and you recognize their vacant, exhausted eyes. You read a missive that pierces your heart. You answer the phone and hear the sighing hello. And on that day, you remember. You remember the ache and disorientation, the taste of bitterness. You see in them something you recognize—and you know better how to love them because you have walked through the valley of the shadow.

These are the moments when we can say with Mother Teresa that we have come to "love the darkness"—not for itself but because it became the training ground to equip us to help another suffering traveler.

7

MARTIN LUTHER KING JR.

Drink from the Reservoir of Resilience

The salty air hung thick around him. He waited out the night, kept company by the rhythm of the waves. They were steady, like a breath—the inhale of water pulled to sea, the rush as it pushed its way to the shore.

They'd sent him here to rest, but sleep evaded him. He was exhausted, battle-weary, his mind a fog of fatigue, but still he lay awake in a strange bed. The sleeping pills no longer worked. He'd listened to his friend Ralph snoring in the bed beside him. That snore had been a companion in the long night of many prison cells.

In an agony of wakefulness, he'd slipped out onto the balcony and now stood staring, unseeing, at the sea. Waves splattered, hungry, against a rock below him. The words of the song came to him unbidden: "Breakers dashing trying to conquer my soul. I heard the voice of Jesus saying still to fight on, he promised never to leave me, never to leave me alone."

But he felt so alone. He thought they would understand when he spoke out against the war. How could he advocate for nonviolence at home when violence decimated the lives of those abroad? The comments from the press were searing, but this was nothing new.

His friends and allies turning on him, though—that cut deep. They'd stopped calling. They'd stopped giving. They'd accused him of distracting from the cause. It was no longer an angry, anonymous voice on the phone at midnight telling him to keep his mouth shut—or else. It was the voice of those he trusted. The loneliness was heavy. He was being abandoned.

The waves glinted silver in the light of the approaching dawn. He heard Ralph stir behind him. His steps were quick with alarm. He could hear it in his voice: "Michael, what's wrong?" He smiled at his friend's use of his childhood name. Dear Ralph. His dearest friend. So much would fall to him when he was gone.

He gestured toward the sound of the crashing waves. "Who put that rock there?" he asked. Who had put *him* here, in the middle of this mess, in the leadership of this movement? "Don't you know what I've been thinking, Ralph?"

"Rock of ages, cleft for me, let me hide myself in Thee." Martin's baritone broke the predawn silence as the words surged from deep within him. He could feel them filling his chest, could feel his throat grow thick with the desperate need for them to be true.

How could he continue this fight? How could he return to take up the weary mantle of leadership again? The waves broke over him—of guilt, of inadequacy, of failure, of destruction. How could he withstand them?

"Nothing in my hands I bring. Simply to Thy cross I cling. . . . While I draw this fleeting breath, when mine eyes shall close in death. . . . Rock of ages, cleft for me, let me hide myself in Thee."

The waves crashed on without end. God alone could give him shelter.[1]

SLEEPLESS IN MONTGOMERY: THE MAKING OF A LEADER

When Martin Luther King Jr.'s lone voice echoed over the waters of Acapulco, Mexico, he was near the end of his earthly journey and in the midst of one of the most difficult seasons of his life. He'd been in the fray of the civil rights movement for about twelve years, since he'd been thrust into leadership at the age of twenty-six while pastor at Dexter Avenue Baptist Church in Montgomery, Alabama. He and his young wife, Coretta, had just welcomed their first child into the world when a seamstress named Rosa Parks refused to give up her seat on a segregated Montgomery bus. Her arrest and indictment had incited the iconic bus boycott. The newly formed Montgomery Improvement Association (MIA) elected King as its president, in spite of his youth, in large part because he was a recent transplant with few ties of partisan allegiance.

From the beginning, he felt awed by the responsibility entrusted to him and unfit for the mammoth task ahead. As he worked on his first speech as the newly elected MIA president, these feelings became overwhelming. He was "almost overcome, obsessed by a feeling of inadequacy." Anxiety paralyzed his mind, blocking the flow of words. In this moment, he turned to prayer, trusting a God "whose matchless strength stands over against the frailties and inadequacies of human nature." He prayed for strength and for guidance—and then started writing. It was a pattern for all that lay ahead.[2]

Months later, as the boycott wore on, he "almost broke down under the continual battering" of arguments that he was too young to lead, that he had pushed local leaders out to become president, that the whole protest was doomed for failure. He couldn't sleep. There seemed to be no choice but to resign. He had barely finished delivering his resignation speech before the board unanimously voted to keep him as president.[3]

Even after he gained worldwide recognition and respect, a sense of inadequacy still plagued King. At times, these feelings simply reflected his humility.[4] At other times, though, especially toward the end of his life and in the low moments, these feelings were the fruit of something bleaker. His close colleague Andrew Young said,

As much as he did, he always blamed himself for not doing enough. He was a kind of workaholic where he was never content. He was driven by a kind of need for perfection. And he was always feeling that he wasn't doing his best. I think because of his feeling that he wasn't good enough to be the leader. Those were periods when he was really just physically exhausted.[5]

In spite of his feelings, good or ill, he bore the mantle of leadership well. The Montgomery bus boycott stretched on for nearly a year, until the US Supreme Court declared Montgomery's segregation laws unconstitutional. It was King's first great victory in the civil rights movement.

His involvement, travels, writing, speaking, and organizing were unceasing over the next decade. I do not have space here to detail all of King's extensive work for the rights and dignity of Black Americans,[6] but I'll highlight a few events. The bus boycotts in Montgomery led to the creation of the Southern Christian Leadership Conference (SCLC), which played an active role in many of the civil rights efforts throughout the 1950s and 1960s.[7] King served as president until his death.

In 1963, nearly eight years after his beginnings in Montgomery, King found himself heavily involved in the freedom work in Birmingham, Alabama, which would become one of the most iconic showdowns of the civil rights era, one that would prick the conscience of a nation.

Later that year, King gave his famous "I Have a Dream" speech in front of the Lincoln Memorial in Washington, DC. The following year, he was named *Time*'s Man of the Year and awarded the Nobel Peace Prize.

This is the Martin Luther King Jr. so many know. The hero. The champion. The strong leader, fighting injustice. But as with all of our heroes, we forget he was human. He was not a perfect man. He was not invincible. Personal and private battles lurked beyond the public stage.

SECRET SADNESS: WHY KING DIDN'T GET HELP

Martin Luther King Jr. did not speak publicly about his depression. This is a great loss for us to not be able to hear firsthand about his experience. This reality also poses a challenge. Since we must piece together King's mental and emotional state, there are times when it's hard to discern if he's discouraged, under pressure, sad, or actually depressed. We've all experienced moments of discouragement or sadness in our circumstances, but this doesn't necessarily mean we're depressed. The same applies here. Separated by time and without his own self-disclosure of his symptoms, it's impossible to know or to diagnose him at all points.

Some have pointed to this as a lack of evidence, particularly as the public face of King was confident and assured. Fortunately, we are not limited by King's public persona, and the accounts from his closest friends, advisers, and colleagues tell a different story than the face under the spotlights. They tell us of King as a young boy, who, overcome with despair and self-blame over the death of his grandmother, twice threw himself from a window in an attempt to take his own life. And they tell us of King's brother, A. D., who wrestled with depression and alcoholism and made repeated suicide threats throughout his adulthood, hinting at a possible family proclivity to depression.

Those close to King attest to a man who was troubled and struggled cyclically with depression. In particular, they point to the last year and a half of his life, when King the hero became one of the most hated men in America and when King's depression sparked concern among those close to him of the need for a psychiatrist.

If King was this depressed, we might ask, why didn't he get help? He is the only person in this book who had access to a semblance of what we consider modern psychiatric care, but he didn't seek it out.

In some ways, this is simply human nature. It's hard to come to the place where we admit we need help, that we can't hold it together by sheer willpower, that our brains have turned against us. I remember how painful it was for me to finally accept the reality of my depression, to stare the darkness in the face and call it by name. I remember my heavy steps as I walked up the hill to my college's counseling center, my friend by my side to make sure I kept my appointment. I remember hoping that no one saw me walking through those doors, afraid of what they might think of me. When the time came, I wrestled against taking medication. Those tiny pills felt like defeat, like failure, like faithlessness. They weren't, of course—but the battle to accept this and accept the help I needed was real.

We also, however, cannot forget King's context as a Black man in America in the 1960s. We know that within the Black community, mental illness is underreported and often misdiagnosed.[8] We can assume this would have been even more true fifty years ago. So even if King would have sought professional help, it's possible he wouldn't have gotten the help he needed. Psychiatric care and the first antidepressants were available, yes, but they were still fairly new and not as advanced as they are now. Their presence did not eliminate the stigma around mental illness. This stigma continues to this day, half a century later.

On top of all these factors is the hard truth that King wasn't free to share about his depression. There was too much at stake. He was the leader of a national movement and the voice for nonviolence, in a fragile position, under attack from all sides. Even a whisper of psychiatric care would have given any of his many opponents ammunition to discredit him. "See, he's crazy," they could say.

And a whisper, if not a bull horn, surely would have announced his psychiatric care to the world. The FBI had so extensively, invasively, and, at times, illegally wiretapped and bugged King's life, that it would have only been a matter of time until they had full documentation of his visits. In fact, one of King's New York doctors did

suggest that he seek the help of a psychiatrist, but it was ruled out
of the question for fear of the FBI's interference.[9]

He didn't have the freedom to share about his struggles publicly. He didn't even have the freedom to seek the help he needed
privately. He had no choice but to carry on.

DRUM MAJOR WITH A SORE THROAT: DEPRESSION AT THE END

King carried on during the last season of his life in a circumstantial
firestorm. He grieved the riots erupting in major cities throughout
the country. These, combined with the rise of the Black Power
movement, which questioned the efficacy of nonviolence and vehe-
mently rejected his attempts to work with White allies, made him
question the future of the nonviolent movement.[10]

He'd been afraid years before, in the aftermath of the Montgomery protests, of peaking too early in his career, of fading into
irrelevancy. And now it felt as if those fears were being realized.[11]
The influence he'd had was slowly slipping away. The new generation of rising Black leaders questioned his authority and his
tactics. Other Black leaders, like those in Chicago, where he'd gone
to help with a housing crisis, wanted him to mind his own business
and not disrupt their communities.[12] He was losing support and
losing momentum.

This shift solidified after he spoke out definitively against the war
in Vietnam in his famous speech at Riverside Church in New York
City. Grieving the violence of the war, he had labored through a
decision to speak out against it—and, in doing so, against the same
president who had been civil rights' greatest ally. His decision
brought the harshest criticism of his life. He lost what had been the
waning support of the White House and was eviscerated in the
papers. Many told him to stay in his place, to not stick his nose
where it didn't belong. Worst of all, even friends turned against him.
This new peace talk was too radical, or it distracted from the cause
of civil rights, or it was traitorous. People stopped talking to him,

stopped inviting him into their pulpits, stopped supporting the work of SCLC. It was these criticisms that hurt King worst of all. He felt abandoned and alone. Xernona Clayton, a close friend and advisor of the Kings, said, "It had bothered him deeply that the nation had turned against him. . . . I always tell people he died of a broken heart."[13]

In the midst of all of this, the usual hectic pace continued, along with the immense pressures of being the figurehead of a national movement, the constant fears that he wasn't good enough to be the leader of it, time away from home, and the invasive and persecuting surveillance of the FBI.[14]

It is no wonder that King's staff and friends became concerned. Their stories alone give us a picture of how depression was eating away at King's psyche, changing his behavior. With the possibility of psychiatric care ruled out, they tried to help as best they could.

The first battle was what his friend Ralph Abernathy called "Martin's war on sleep."[15] King was tired. He'd been going nonstop for thirteen years. At first, it had been his frenetic pace that stole his sleep. Over time, insomnia took a deeper hold on him. He was prescribed sleeping pills. When they stopped working, his aides thought he needed a "more drastic psychiatric approach."[16]

They were probably right. Exhaustion and depression feed each other. Depression causes fatigue and sleeplessness, that purgatory of exhausted wakefulness. Lack of sleep can exacerbate depression symptoms. King was caught up in this vicious cycle. As time continued, he grew more and more sleep-deprived and more and more despondent.

Aides and friends, fully aware of his sleeplessness and the underlying depression it often pointed to, would sometimes stay up with him, "[running] relays keeping him company" through the early morning hours, talking with him about whatever was on his mind.[17] They couldn't cure his depression or lull him into restful slumber. But they could stay up and talk.

They also tried to make him laugh. As what would be King's final birthday drew near, his staff grew alarmed as they saw his typically abundant sense of humor shriveling. They called Xernona Clayton and said, "We haven't seen him laugh in a long time. Think of something to do to make him laugh."[18] Xernona therefore compiled a set of gag gifts for King, in honor of his birthday: a can of shoestring potatoes, for when he had his shoestrings taken in jail, and a cup that said, "We are cooperating with Lyndon Johnson's war on poverty. Drop coins and bills in the cup." In a video recording of the presentation of these gifts, it's evident Xernona achieved her goal—King laughs loudly, enjoying the joke.

As King's staff and friends saw his laughter drying up, they also saw his temper begin to flare. In the past, he was always calm and quiet in feisty staff meetings as staff debated strategy. A fatherlike figure, he would listen carefully, asking just the right questions, quick with patience and understanding. But that began to change. He started erupting in anger, and his staff bore the brunt of it.

At one infamous staff meeting, shortly before King's murder, his SCLC staff were divided and bickering over their next projects. King wanted to go to Memphis, to support the sanitation workers' strike going on there, but his staff disagreed. They were already stretched thin with the Poor People's Campaign, an ambitious plan for thousands to converge on Washington, DC, to draw attention to the nation's poor of all races. One person thought he should focus more on the Vietnam peace movement. Finally, King lost it and started yelling. This was unheard of. After ripping into several staff members, he stormed out of the meeting, ignoring their pleas as they chased after him down the hallway. He disappeared for several hours.

Exhausted and morose, King began to talk more of his own death. It seemed a thought unshakable from his mind. The possibility of his own early demise was a reality he'd wrestled with since his days in Montgomery, when he and his family received death threats by phone and mail constantly and when his home was bombed. He'd also been stabbed in New York City ten years before his assassination, and doctors later told him that the blade was so close to his aorta that if he'd merely sneezed he'd have died.[19] He had stared death in the face and told many of his close friends and staff that he had come to terms with it. But in those last few months, he started speaking of it more publicly.

In his last sermon at Ebenezer Baptist Church, where he'd copastored with his father for years, King ruminated on what he'd want to be said at his funeral in his famous "Drum Major Instinct" sermon. Two months after he originally delivered the sermon, his voice crackled from a recording of it to the many gathered for his funeral.

On the night before his assassination, he delivered his final speech for a rally in Memphis, Tennessee, for the sanitation workers' strike. It was a speech delivered without notes or preparation, and one that almost didn't happen. He was exhausted, had a sore throat, and didn't think many would come because of an intense storm. He didn't feel like talking, he said. So he stayed at his hotel and went to bed. When Ralph Abernathy and King's colleague Jesse Jackson arrived at the rally to find a large crowd disappointed at King's absence, they called and insisted he come.

One biographer calls the speech "darkly pessimistic" and "soul searching as he contemplated the specter of death."[20] King quickly turned to the theme of his own mortality. He told the story of the bomb threat on his recent plane ride to Memphis and of the death threats that welcomed him upon his arrival. He told the story of his stabbing and of a little girl's kind note that she was "so glad he didn't sneeze." Then his comments took on an eerily prophetic turn.

> Like anybody, I would like to live a long life—longevity has its place. But I'm not concerned about that now. I just want to do God's will. And He's allowed me to go up to the mountain. And I've looked over, and I've seen the Promised Land. I may not get there with you. But I want you to know tonight, that we, as a

people, will get to the Promised Land. And so I'm happy to-night; I'm not worried about anything; I'm not fearing any man. Mine eyes have seen the glory of the coming of the Lord.[21]

He abruptly turned and staggered away from the podium. After the fact, his wife Coretta thought he became so emotional that he couldn't finish the stanza of the song he was quoting.[22] He seems to have either collapsed or lost his footing and fallen into the arms of Ralph Abernathy, who lowered him unsteadily into a chair. A lawyer in attendance that night said, "It was as though somebody had taken a beach ball and pulled the plug out, as if all his energy had been sucked out."[23] He was spent.

And yet he didn't want to leave. Usually he slipped out quickly to avoid being crushed by an overwhelming crowd. But on that night, he wanted to stay and talk to the people.[24] It was his last chance to do so. The next day, an assassin's bullet would claim his life.

DRINKING DEEP FROM THE RESERVOIR

When I began my study of Dr. King, I thought I knew what he had to teach me. But as I read his words, listened to his resonate voice, and absorbed the accounts of his behavior and attitude, I found something much deeper than what I first thought. It was more raw, robust, and human than the tidied-up, storybook version of him. I saw the pressure and danger he faced—enough to make any person crumble psychologically. I heard of the depression and anxiety he battled and kept hidden. And I began to see a pattern. He faced hard circumstances—and he was not impervious to their attack—but he had tools to anchor him, to give him the strength and hope he needed to survive. They provided a deep and abiding source he could pull from to stare down evil, death threats, discouragement, and even the attacks of his own psyche. It was a reservoir of resilience.

Laughing at the nightmare: reservoir of humor. I know of at least one biographer of King who claims that reports of him being depressed are exaggerated, for how could someone have such a sense of humor and struggle with depression? When I repeated this justification to one Black pastor and scholar, he simply laughed. Humor sometimes is not about a jolly, happy-go-lucky spirit. It allows people to laugh at the very thing that causes them pain or represents their greatest terror. It's a way to cope, a way to survive.[25]

King was known for his sense of humor, and we can see how he used it to keep his demons at bay. He and his fellow civil rights workers knew the threat they were under. Being a Black man in the South was already a dangerous position. Lynchings happened with impunity. Their vocal support and organization of the civil rights movement painted a target on their backs. They saw friends and fellow activists murdered. They knew the risks were real.

Enter King with his reservoir of humor. "Now, Andy," he would say to Andrew Young, "when you do something foolish and you go out there and get assassinated, I promise, I'm gonna preach the best funeral for you." Off he would go, preaching a satirical eulogy, highlighting Young's (or whoever else was the lucky recipient) faults and quirks. Before long, he had everyone laughing—at a real life-and-death situation. His friend C. T. Vivian said, "Martin joked about it [death] because there wasn't any other way to be."[26]

How did he cope with the unimaginable pressure he was under? How did he cope with the threat of death? How did he cope with the nightmares of depression's gloom? He found some way to mock them. He found some way to laugh. And because of this humor, albeit grim, he was not overcome.

"Joshua fit the battle": reservoir of song. Martin Luther King Jr. came from a heritage rich in music. The spirituals and gospel songs he so often repeated and sang with his fellow civil rights laborers encouraged him, as they did the slaves who were his ancestors. The lyrics gave King—and those within the Black community and beyond—a language of hope. Not a spurious hope, blind to life's sorrows, but a hope that could stare down the horrors of hell itself

and not give way. It was a hope grounded in God's power in justice and liberation and his presence with the oppressed. It was a hope that knew God could make a way out of no way.[27]

The songs, sung by the determined voices of civil rights workers and the haunting voices of gospel singers like King's friend Mahalia Jackson, wove a soundtrack around the civil rights movement. They provided a reservoir of hope from which King could draw deeply when he was discouraged, frightened—or depressed. He pointed others to this reservoir as well, turning to the language of the spirituals in his sermons.

Once, when King and his colleagues were working in Mississippi, he was exhausted and depressed. No matter what his friends and aides tried, they could not get him out of bed. He refused to get up. Life felt too exhausting, too daunting. He wanted to stay under the covers and simply disappear for a while. He longed for the numbing emptiness of sleep. (Have you been there?) But King had obligations. He was to escort a group of little girls to integrate an elementary school.

Andrew Young went to find Joan Baez, a folk singer and close friend of King's, and begged her to come sing for him. Baez agreed, pushing through the anxious onlookers at the minister's home where King was staying and entering his room. Then she began to sing:

> I am a poor pilgrim of sorrow
> I'm traveling this wide world alone
> No hope have I for tomorrow
> I'm trying to make heaven my home.
> Sometimes I'm tossed and driven
> Sometimes I don't know where to roam.
> But I've heard of a city called heaven,
> And I'm trying to make it my home.[28]

She continued on, singing the verses of the old gospel song she'd learned from a woman at the Sixteenth Street Baptist Church in

Birmingham only a few years before.[29] It was a church community that knew the taste of sorrow, as it had lost the lives of four precious little girls in a bombing during the civil rights struggle there.

The words floated around the room in Baez's unaccompanied soprano voice. By the second or third verse, King began to smile faintly. When she finished, he got up, completed his personal grooming routine, and went off to do his business.[30] It was the song's medicine that reached him when nothing else could. It was the song that got him out of bed.

That same year, King found himself in Chicago, engaged in a struggle for fair housing, a struggle that became one of the most discouraging of his career. The violence and racism in this northern city surprised him and his coworkers, as did the harsh resistance of its Black leaders to SCLC's involvement. In a video of one of the rallies held there, Mahalia Jackson appears with King. He has stepped into the pulpit and is preparing to speak to the large crowd gathered at the Vernon Park Church of God in Christ when Mahalia suddenly bursts into song. It appears impromptu, as if she's returned to her seat, only to launch into one more song. You can see a man scurry across the stage and thrust a small microphone into her hand.

As soon as King hears the first words, he grins slightly. As she carries on, the crowd sings loudly with her, clapping in rhythm and getting to their feet. They've caught the spirit of the song. King's grin grows into a full, face-splitting smile. He nods his head. He gets it. Mahalia is preaching to him, as much as she's preaching to the crowd. Did she look over and see his face as he was about to begin? Did she see how serious he looked, how discouraged? Did she know he was depressed?

Mahalia Jackson was preaching a message of hope through the words of an old spiritual: "Joshua fit the battle of Jericho, Jericho, Jericho. Joshua fit the battle of Jericho, and the walls came tumbling down." Even when the battle seems hopeless, even when the forces against you seem too large to overcome, this is not the end of the story. With God on your side, any battle can be won. He fights for you, and he can make a way out of no way.[31]

When I see King's smiling face in that video, I see a man being encouraged, nodding his head as if to say, "I hear you, Mahalia. I hear you. And I receive."

He was drinking from the reservoir. The culture of the American Black church had provided and preserved it for him. It was there to drink from each time he grew discouraged, each time depression tempted him to despair and give up entirely. It allowed him to live with reality but also with hope. It provided a way for him to not be overcome.

"God had been my cellmate": reservoir of spirituality. Closely related to this reservoir of song was the resilience given to King through spirituality. Foundational to his spirituality was a sense of "cosmic companionship." He had a deep and abiding sense of a God who was with his people in the midst of life's darkest midnights.

King found himself in one such midnight during the early days in Montgomery. He was awake in the middle of the night, the words of a threatening phone call echoing in his ears. As he sat at the kitchen table with a cup of coffee in his hands, he thought of his wife and his newborn daughter, of what would happen if one of those angry voices successfully carried through on their threats. What would happen if he lost them? If they lost him? The weight of the struggle seemed too much to bear. He felt weak. He wondered how he could carry on.

And then he knew what to do—what his daddy had taught him. He bowed his head over his steaming cup and began to pray. He was weak, he said, and losing courage. He was at the end of himself, with nothing left. So he turned to One with power and strength, the One who could "make a way out of no way." In that moment of desperate prayer, in that midnight at a kitchen table in Montgomery, God met him. King felt the assurance of his presence: "At that moment I experienced the presence of the Divine as I had never experienced Him before. Almost at once my fears began to go. My uncertainty disappeared. I was ready to face anything."[32]

Several months before he was killed, during that season in which he felt abandoned, alone, and adrift, he preached at Ebenezer Baptist Church about Shadrach, Meshach, and Abednego (Daniel 3). As he reflected on the divine companion who appears with these three brave young men in the fiery furnace, he encouraged the congregation (and himself): "Don't ever think you're by yourself. Go on to jail if necessary, but you'll never go alone. Take a stand for that which is right, and the world may misunderstand you and criticize you, but you never go alone." He ended by quoting the words of a popular song: "Yes, I've seen the lightning flash; I've heard the thunder roll; I've felt sin's breakers dashing trying to conquer my soul, but I heard the voice of Jesus saying still to fight on; he promised never to leave me, never to leave me alone; no, never alone, no, never alone. He promised never to leave me, never to leave me alone."[33]

He'd learned this lesson years earlier in a jail cell in Birmingham, where he was kept for over twenty-four hours in solitary confinement, kept even from contact with his lawyers. While he wasn't physically abused, his mind was tortured. Worry consumed him. About the movement. About the others in jail. About his life and his family. Later, he said,

> Those were the longest, most frustrating and bewildering hours I have lived. . . . In the mornings the sun would rise, sending shafts of light through the window high in the narrow cell which was my home. You will never know the meaning of utter darkness until you have lain in such a dungeon, knowing that sunlight is streaming overhead and still seeing only darkness below. You might have thought I was in the grip of a fantasy brought on by worry. I did worry. But there was more to the blackness than a phenomenon conjured up by a worried

mind. Whatever the cause, the fact remained that I could not see the light.[34]

When he was finally allowed to see his lawyer, he found out that his dear friend Harry Belafonte had been able to raise a large sum of money to bail out other protesters, which had been an overwhelming concern for King. In that moment, the true nature of his situation became clear to him:

> I had never been truly in solitary confinement. God's companionship does not stop at the door of a jail cell. God had been my cellmate. . . . In the midst of deepest midnight, daybreak had come. I did not know whether the sun was shining at that moment. But I knew that once again I could see the light.[35]

God's companionship does not stop at the door of a jail cell. God had been my cellmate. By the end of his life, King could add even more to this wisdom. God's companionship does not stop with the murder of friends, with the thwarting of justice, with the harshest criticism and slander. His companionship does not stop when we make mistakes or in the moment when we stare death in the face. He is our cellmate with fear, exhaustion, and depression. He promised never to leave us alone.

• • •

King's resilience reservoir was nurtured by his culture as a Black American. It had been well-prepared and oft-tested by his ancestors through decades of slavery, segregation, racism, violence, and hatred. The faith, the spirituals, the humor were hard-won gifts given to him by them—and they enabled him to survive.

Resilience enables us to hold on to hope in the midst of life's pain—even the pain hidden within our minds. It allows us to carry on, to rebound, to be "struck down, but not destroyed" (2 Corinthians 4:9). For some of us, it comes naturally. Our culture, family, or life circumstances may have taught us early on how to not let pain have the last word. For others of us, it's something we must learn, cultivate, and practice. Our arsenal must be pieced together as we go.

Like King, you may draw from the reservoirs of humor, music, or spirituality. You may draw from the support of family and friends, as I did, and find their love to be a buoy. These reservoirs don't remove the pain. They don't instantly dissipate the heavy fog of depression from our minds. But they do give us anchors, sure and strong, to hold us fast until the light begins to dawn again.

CONCLUSION

The Water Is Deep, but the Bottom Is Good

Mother Teresa once said, "If I ever become a saint, I will surely be one of darkness."[1] When we look back on her life, it's clear that the darkness she endured shaped her into the saint we celebrate today. We can see its fire purifying her, making her holy, teaching her of God's character. It left its mark on her as she came into contact with the invisible One who abided with her in her suffering, the One who was familiar with sorrow and "acquainted with grief" (Isaiah 53:3). We can see that for all of our brothers and sisters in this book.

We call them saints not because they were perfect or superhuman— they were normal people, much like you and me. Their experience was not much different from ours. It merely occurred in a different time and place. They felt heartache. They had doubts. They made mistakes. They grew in their understanding of God and themselves. They stumbled in their attempts to follow him well.

And they were depressed. They drank the cup of that bitterness, knew its horrors, and battled its demons—just as I have, and perhaps you have as well. But they were saints who followed Jesus as Savior and Lord, who were ever growing in their formation as his disciples.

Their stories are not just about learning to follow Jesus in the darkness, however. Mother Teresa meant more than that in her words. She explained that she would be present to bring light to the darkness of those on the earth. She would be a saint for their darkness. One to guide them through the pain.

This is the true power of the stories of these friends I've come to know over the years. They are guides and companions through the darkness of depression. They offer a little light on the way. Not a light from themselves but a light reflecting the God who met them—even when they couldn't see it.

We need their encouragement. We need the hope they remind us of. We need to embrace the wisdom they offer.

• • •

In one of his many references to *The Pilgrim's Progress*, Charles Spurgeon describes the story of Christian and his companion Hopeful as they cross the River of Death. Christian fears he will be swept under, but Hopeful holds him up. "Fear not—I feel the bottom," he says. Spurgeon saw in this image a metaphor for our trials. Our fellow companions and our Savior himself hold us up in the midst of the waves and encourage us: "Fear not! The water may be deep, but the bottom is good."[2]

The water is deep, yes—its murky depths may strike terror in your soul. Its currents might pull at you, threatening to drag you under to its watery grave. It may sap your strength, making you wonder if you can—or even want to—carry on. But the bottom is good. Keep taking one more step, no matter how faltering or hesitant. Your foot will find a place to land.

We need people who can hold us up during our struggles with depression. We need people who can shout back to us from further ahead. Depression is a fierce enemy, they say, but it need not be your victor. It need not have the last say. Your usefulness is not over. Your God has not left you. The water is deep, but the bottom is good.

And don't think that only those whose stories make it into the history books can offer this encouragement, my friend. You can too.

You, too, have stories to share. Stories of the darkness, yes, but also of how it shaped you, of how you survived. You, too, can be a guide for others through the dark, a companion in the deepest night. You, too, can bring a flicker of light to another suffering soul. And some day, someone may look back at you and declare you also to be in this sacred company—a saint of darkness.

ACKNOWLEDGMENTS

This book exists because of the support, encouragement, and insight I've gained from many people, to whom I owe thanks and gratitude.

To the friends who have been listening to me talk about this book in various forms for years—you know who you are. You have been tireless in your support, your willingness to listen to my verbal processing, your genuine interest, your editorial feedback, and your cups of tea. You are my earliest pro bono marketing team, and I cannot thank you enough for believing in this, praying for me, and cheering me along.

To the brave few who read early versions of my manuscript, especially Susan and Kelvin Anderson, Ethan Clever, Katelyn and Drew Dixon, and Mary Lou Jones for being enthusiastic and thoughtful beta readers.

To Patrick Smith for your valuable insight on Dr. King, and to Josina Guess and Byron Borger for book recommendations.

To my friends and colleagues at Gordon-Conwell Theological Seminary. To the Goddard library staff for cheerfully caring for my stacks of research materials. To the Tuesday Table crew for being a sounding board, a place to process, laugh, and rest on long research days. You helped to bring shape to my thoughts in several chapters. And to Gwenfair Adams for introducing me to the first of these stories.

To the wonderful folks at IVP, especially to my editor, Ethan McCarthy, for making this a better book, to Lori Neff for her marketing prowess, and to David Fassett for a cover that brought tears to my eyes. And to my "publishing champion," Jeff Crosby, who believed in this project in its earliest form.

To my parents, Barry and Mandy Stottlemyer, for being my faithful readers, editors, and cheerleaders from the beginning, and to my in-laws, Wayne and Stacy Gruver, for gifting me that writing conference.

To Scott, for taking a risk on an unlikely dream, for your steady encouragement, and for the sacrifices and support that have made this possible. I love you.

And to the friends who walked with me through dark days—you were the steady presence of God to me. I can write this book because of your faithful friendship.

APPENDIX

When One You Love Is in the Dark

To be sure, his deliverance would be to me one of the greatest blessings my thoughts can conceive.

JOHN NEWTON OF HIS FRIEND
WILLIAM COWPER

I know some of you reading this book are not depressed yourselves but have a loved one who is. They may be a family member, a friend, or perhaps a parishioner or student under your care.

It's horrible to watch someone you care about suffer. I usually see it in the eyes. They look dull, like the spark of life has drained from them. Or in the muscles of their face trying to remember how to smile. Looking into that face, it's easy to feel powerless to do anything to help.

Depression—and mental illness in general—feels particularly scary to many of us. We don't know where to start. So I'd like to share some practical things you can do to help those who are depressed around you.

1. KNOW WHAT DEPRESSION LOOKS LIKE.

It's challenging to help with depression if you don't know the warning signs. Familiarize yourself with the symptoms. The classic signs of depression are persistent sadness and hopelessness and a loss of interest in once-pleasurable things or activities. Your loved one may cry but not know why. He may shrug off playing that game or going to that movie. She may see everything in the worst light—and have no hope that life will get better. Depression also bears physical signs, like unexplained aches and pains, and cognitive signs, like difficulty concentrating or indecisiveness. It often involves sleep disturbances—insomnia or oversleeping—and eating disturbances—overeating or lack of appetite. Other things to watch out for are irritability, fatigue, pervading guilt or worthlessness, and reckless behavior. If your loved one has struggled with depression in the past, observe how these symptoms typically manifest in his or her life to keep an eye out for recurring episodes.

The National Alliance on Mental Illness (NAMI) is an excellent educational resource where you can learn more: www.nami.org.

2. SUGGEST PROFESSIONAL HELP.

Some people may not recognize depression for what it is. Share with them gently what you've observed and suggest they seek help to get well. Remind them that depression is an illness and not something to be ashamed of. Encourage them to see a professional, such as a licensed counselor, their primary care physician, or a mental health care provider. It's a good idea to have a list of trusted counselors or providers in your area to help someone get started—particularly if you are a pastor, youth worker, teacher, or other people-helper.

3. BE A COMPASSIONATE LISTENER.

Calmly and compassionately listen when the person wants to talk about how they're feeling. Ask good, open-ended questions that give them space to share about their experience. Avoid responding immediately with advice, opinions, judgment, or dismissive comments. Instead, focus on providing a safe environment for them to share, and seek to understand how they are feeling. Keep the lines of communication open.

4. PROVIDE PRACTICAL SUPPORT.

Depression interferes with everyday tasks and can make even the simplest of things feel overwhelming. If the person is in your household, create ways to help them manage day-to-day tasks and encourage their autonomy as much as they are able. If they aren't under your roof, look for ways you can offer practical support to ease this burden for the person or for their family. Bring a meal. Offer to do laundry. Provide a ride to doctor's appointments. Cover childcare during counseling sessions.

Practical support may also include inviting them to do something, such as seeing a movie, going for a walk, or participating in a hobby they once enjoyed. It's okay if they turn you down—continue to extend these invitations for them to engage in simple life-giving activities.

5. PRAY.

Pray for God's healing—whether through the intervention of doctors and medicine or through supernatural means. Pray that they can connect with a counselor with whom they can develop a strong relationship. Pray for God's protection over them. Pray for wisdom to know the best ways to love and support them, for discernment to know when to sit in silence and when to speak, when to push them toward the next step and when to listen.

6. ENCOURAGE SPIRITUAL PRACTICES APPROPRIATE FOR THIS SEASON.

Depression may cause a shift in a person's practice of spiritual disciplines. Help them find and engage in spiritual practices that cultivate faith, hope, and an awareness of the gospel in this season. You might suggest things like communal prayer or journaling. Remind them of the truths of the gospel—of God's unrelenting work to redeem and restore, of his never-ending grace, of our hope that he is making all things new. Point them to passages and sections of

Scripture that dwell on God's presence with the brokenhearted or how he worked through the pain of people in the Bible. Praying and meditating on the lament psalms is also an excellent practice and may provide freedom and language for their prayers.

7. CELEBRATE LITTLE VICTORIES.

Healing from depression may come in fits and starts. Be on the lookout for ways your loved one is taking initiative in their own wellness or making improvements. Encourage and celebrate these steps, no matter how small. Maybe they made it out of bed today. Maybe they're regularly taking their meds. Maybe they made it out of the house. Maybe they put into practice a coping technique from their therapist. Help them to see these little victories for what they are—and rejoice.

8. DON'T BE AFRAID TO ASK ABOUT SUICIDE.

Suicide is serious business. Many people are afraid to ask about it and dance around the topic, concerned that they will plant the idea in someone's mind. There is no evidence that asking directly about suicide and suicidal thoughts increases a person's risk. In fact, the opposite seems to be true. Do not be afraid to ask someone directly if they are having thoughts of self-harm or suicide. And don't be sworn to secrecy about suicidal thoughts or plans—it's important to get help for a person at risk.

Know what to do if you believe someone to be at risk of suicide. You can call the National Suicide Prevention Lifeline yourself at 1-800-273-8255 or chat with them on their website at https://suicidepreventionlifeline.org. Or you can help the person you love call them. If you believe someone to be at risk of imminent harm, don't be afraid to call 911 or take them to the emergency room.

9. TAKE CARE OF YOURSELF.

Caring for someone with depression is a marathon, not a sprint. It can be draining, frustrating, and exhausting, even if you deeply love the person and are committed to helping them. Burning out or threatening your own mental health will greatly limit your ability to be helpful for another person. Practice good self-care and maintain your physical, spiritual, and mental health. If the person who is struggling is particularly close to you, such as your spouse or a child, you may want to seek counseling for yourself to process what you're going through.

Don't be a lone ranger—that is a recipe for burnout. Caring for someone with a mental illness should be a team effort, not something you do alone. Make sure there are other support systems and individuals in place for the person you're caring for so that you can have the freedom to take a step back to regroup or refresh yourself.

10. KEEP SHOWING UP.

Walking with someone through depression is often a long process. It therefore requires patience and perseverance. It can be easy to give up or pull back when healing becomes a journey and not an instant fix. But keep showing up. Keep checking in to see how the person is doing. Keep inviting them to do things. Keep sitting with them until the light returns. Your repeated loving support is an important part of the healing process.

BRIEF BIOGRAPHIES OF
THE COMPANIONS

MARTIN LUTHER (1483–1546)

Martin Luther, the German Protestant Reformer, was born in Eisleben on November 10, 1483. In 1501, he entered the University of Erfurt, on track for a career in law. In 1505, he abandoned his studies and entered an Augustinian monastery and then was ordained as a priest in 1507. He was sent to study at the University of Wittenberg, where he received his doctorate in theology in 1512 and became a professor of theology at the university. His extensive studies of and meditations on the Scriptures—including the Psalms, Romans, Galatians, and Hebrews—in preparation for his lectures slowly began to influence his theology. He came to understand salvation as something not found through good works or acts of penance but only by God's grace through faith in Jesus.

In 1517, Luther published his Ninety-Five Theses as a scholarly objection to the sale of indulgences. Over the following years, the situation escalated as Luther was called to several debates and hearings—and his own theology continued to develop. He was ordered to recant his views, which by that point clearly undermined the pope's authority and questioned accepted theology. When he refused, Luther was excommunicated from the church in 1521. German authorities convened the Diet of Worms, where he was declared an outlaw and a condemned heretic. With the help of friends, he fled and hid in Wartburg Castle, where he translated the New Testament into German.

Luther returned to Wittenberg about a year later in order to calm radical and violent expressions of his teachings. The blossoming Protestant Reformation began to take on not only theological issues but also political ones. In 1524, the Peasants' War began, which Luther harshly condemned.

He married a former nun, Katharina von Bora, in 1525. Katharina was resourceful and a well-suited partner for Luther. They had six children together. Their home in Wittenberg, where they housed boarders, was a hub of conversation, as recorded in Luther's *Table Talk*.

Luther continued to teach at Wittenberg University, where he served as dean of theology from 1533 until his death, and he continued to advise the expanding Reformation. He debated the role and interpretation of the sacraments, crafted a catechism, wrote hymns, preached, and finished his German translation of the Bible. In his final years, he also issued harsh indictments against Anabaptists, the pope, and Jews.

The last decade of Luther's life was fraught with health problems, including heart and digestive problems, kidney stones, and arthritis. Luther died on February 18, 1546.

Suggested Reading

Bainton, Roland H. *Here I Stand: A Life of Martin Luther*. Nashville: Abingdon Press, 1950.

Luther, Martin. *Letters of Spiritual Counsel*. Edited and translated by Theodore G. Tappert. Philadelphia: Westminster Press, 1955.

Luther, Martin. *Table Talk*. Edited and translated by William Hazlitt. London: Fount, 1995.

HANNAH ALLEN (1638–?)

Hannah Allen was born Hannah Archer in Snelston of Derbyshire, England, in 1638. Her father died when she was young. Around the age of twelve, she was sent to London for her education and lived with her aunt. She records her first experience with depression during her teenage years.

In 1655, she married Hannibal Allen, a merchant who was often at sea, and they had a son together before his untimely death around 1663. Hannibal's death sent Hannah, already prone to melancholy, into a deep, suicidal depression that would last for several years. She suffered from religious delusions and a desire to starve herself. Hannah was visited by the minister John Shorthose in the spring of 1666, and his help spurred the beginning of her gradual recovery. In 1668, fully recovered, Hannah married Charles Hatt.

Her spiritual memoir, *[Satan, his Methods and Malice baffled:] A Narrative of God's gracious dealings with Mrs. Hannah Allen . . .*, chronicled her conversion, depression, and recovery. It was published in 1683 by John Wallis after her death, the date of which is unknown. Though she was not the leader or figurehead of a movement, her memoir serves as an enduring picture of the life of an everyday Christian in seventeenth-century England.

Suggested Reading

Lundy, Michael S., ed. *Depression, Anxiety, and the Christian Life: Practical Wisdom from Richard Baxter*. Wheaton, IL: Crossway, 2018.

DAVID BRAINERD (1718–1747)

David Brainerd, a missionary to Native Americans, was born in Haddam, Connecticut, on April 20, 1718. His father and mother both died in his youth. In 1739, he entered Yale, planning to become a minister. He was expelled from Yale in 1742, amid the fervor of the Great Awakening, because of his comments about a tutor. After his expulsion, he lived and studied with Jedidiah Mills in Ripton,

Connecticut, and was eventually appointed a missionary by the Society in Scotland for Propagating Christian Knowledge.

In the spring of 1743, Brainerd began training with John Sergeant in Stockbridge, Massachusetts, and then was sent to his first posting at Kaunaumeek, near modern-day Albany, New York. He would go on to have postings at the Forks of the Delaware in 1744 (near current Easton, Pennsylvania) and in Crossweeksung, New Jersey, from 1745 to 1747. He also took missionary trips into the Susquehanna region, eventually including Native brothers and sisters from the fledgling congregation in New Jersey as fellow evangelists.

Brainerd was discouraged by a lack of visible results during much of his ministry, but during his time in Crossweeksung, he saw a response that he likened to a revival. He remained with that newly formed congregation from 1745 to 1747 and was part of their relocation to Cranberry, New Jersey. After his death, his brother John carried on his ministry there.

After battling tuberculosis since his days at Yale, Brainerd, extremely ill, left his congregation in 1747. He temporarily lived with Jonathan Dickinson, one of the founders of Princeton College (now Princeton University). Brainerd's expulsion from Yale was credited with contributing to its founding, and he has been called Princeton's first student because of his time at Dickinson's home. He then went to live with Jonathan Edwards and his family in Northampton, Massachusetts. Brainerd died there on October 9, 1747, at the age of twenty-nine.

During his time as a missionary, Brainerd published two public journals, at the behest of his missionary society, with reports on his ministry. The first of these was published in 1746, and the second in 1748, after his death. He also kept private journals, which detail his depression, spiritual life, and innermost thoughts. These private diaries were edited, compiled, and published by Jonathan Edwards in 1749. Brainerd's diaries have inspired generations of missionaries and Christians.

Suggested Reading

Brainerd, David. *The Life and Diary of David Brainerd.* Edited by Jonathan Edwards. Middletown, DE: ReadaClassic, 2010.

WILLIAM COWPER (1731–1800)

The English poet and hymnwriter William Cowper (pronounced Cooper) was born on November 26, 1731. His father was a rector, and his mother, who died just before his sixth birthday, was a descendent of the poet John Donne. He wrote of the enduring effects of her loss much later in life in a poem called "On the Receipt of My Mother's Picture." As a child, he attended a boarding school, where he was severely bullied.

While a student of law in London, Cowper suffered his first serious bouts of depression. He recovered from the first, which began in 1752, and went on to finish his degree. He fell in love with his cousin, Theodora, and the two were briefly engaged before her father intervened and broke off the engagement. Neither of them ever married.

In 1763, under the pressure caused by an upcoming public examination for a new job appointment to the House of Lords, Cowper experienced a severe mental breakdown and attempted suicide multiple times. He spent the next eighteen months at a small asylum, St. Albans, under the care of Dr. Cotton, where he eventually recovered and converted to evangelical Christianity. These experiences are recorded in his memoir of his early life.

Cowper moved to Huntingdon in 1765, where he met the Unwin family and became a boarder in their home. The mother, Mary Unwin, remained his dear friend and companion until her death decades later. In 1767, Cowper and the Unwins moved to Olney to be under the ministry of Reverend John Newton. Newton recruited Cowper to help him write a series of hymns, published as the *Olney Hymns* in 1779.

During the winter of 1773–1774, Cowper experienced his third mental breakdown, which included a dream that he believed declared his eternal damnation. He never fully recovered.

Although he had been writing poems since his days in law school, Cowper began in earnest in 1779. His first volume of poetry was published in 1782, and his second, *The Task,* from which we inherited the phrase "variety is the spice of life," was published in 1785. He also published numerous stand-alone poems during his lifetime, including "The Diverting History of John Gilpin" and "The Castaway." His poetry included several anti-slavery poems, and his most famous, "The Negro's Complaint," was quoted by Martin Luther King Jr. Cowper became one of the most popular poets of his day and, with his vivid descriptions of the English countryside, a forerunner of the Romantics. In addition to his poetry, Cowper left behind an extensive collection of letters, which give great insight into his interior life, depression, and creative process.

In 1784, he began translating Homer's *Iliad* and *Odyssey* into blank verse, a project he would devote the next five years of his life to. He moved with Mary Unwin to Weston in 1786 and experienced intermittent mental illness. In 1791, Mary experienced a series of strokes, and as her physical health and his mental health continued to decline, they moved to live with Cowper's relatives in Norfolk in 1795. She died the following year. By the time of her death, Cowper's depression had returned full force and continued through the end of his life, including hallucinations and delusions. He died on April 25, 1800, at the home of his cousin.

Suggested Reading

Cowper, William. "Lines Written During a Fit of Insanity." www.poetry foundation.org/poems/50600/hatred-and-vengeance-my-eternal-portion

Cowper, William. *Selected Poetry and Prose.* Edited by Lyle David Jeffrey. Vancouver, BC: Regent College Publishing, 2007.

CHARLES SPURGEON (1834–1892)

The "Prince of Preachers," Charles Haddon Spurgeon, was born on June 19, 1834, in Essex, England. Spurgeon's formal education was limited, but he was a lifelong learner and avid reader. At his death, his personal library contained over twelve thousand books.

At age fifteen, in 1850, Spurgeon was baptized and became a Baptist (contrary to his family's tradition). The following year, at age sixteen, he gave his first sermon and took up his first pastorate. In 1854, Spurgeon began his ministry at New Park Street Chapel in London. He would serve this congregation until his death. The church grew rapidly, and in 1861, they opened the new Metropolitan Tabernacle with seating for nearly five thousand. Spurgeon was a dynamic preacher, which won him great popularity and great criticism. During his lifetime, his sermons were printed weekly and widely circulated. By the time of his death, he had preached nearly thirty-six hundred sermons.

In 1856, Spurgeon married his wife, Susannah, and later that year they welcomed twin sons. Susannah and Charles both developed chronic health problems. By her early thirties, she was largely an invalid and could not attend her husband's services or travel. By 1869, Spurgeon was already suffering from gout, which left him in great pain and often led him to travel to the more temperate climate of Menton, France, to convalesce.

In addition to his numerous sermons and his pastoral duties, Spurgeon founded a Pastor's College, an orphanage, and a magazine called *The Sword and the Trowel*. He wrote a commentary of the Psalms (*The Treasury of David*), lectures for his ministerial students, devotionals, and countless letters.

In 1887, Spurgeon became embroiled in the "Downgrade Controversy" after he accused some Baptist leaders of "downgrading" Christian doctrine by giving up what he considered to be essentials of the faith in favor of modern, liberal theology. He withdrew his congregation from the Baptist Union and, in turn, was ultimately censured by the Union in 1888.

The city of London went into mourning over his death on January 31, 1892, in Menton. After he died, Susannah compiled his autobiography from letters, vignettes, articles, sermons, and other writings he had recorded.

Suggested Reading

Eswine, Zack. *Spurgeon's Sorrows: Realistic Hope for Those Who Suffer from Depression.* Fearn, Scotland: Christian Focus, 2014.

Spurgeon, Charles. "The Minister's Fainting Fits." In *Lectures to My Students,* 171-83. Albany, OR: Ages Digital Library, 1996.

MOTHER TERESA (1910–1997)

Mother Teresa, the Saint of Calcutta, was born Agnes Gonxha Bojaxhiu on August 26, 1910, in Skopje (now the capital of North Macedonia). Her parents were of Albanian descent. At age twelve, she felt called to the religious life and wanted to become a missionary. In 1928, at eighteen, she left home to join the Sisters of Loreto in Ireland. After a brief training in Dublin, she was sent to Darjeeling, India. She took her first religious vows in 1931 and took the name Mary Teresa. She then went to St. Mary's High School in Calcutta, where she taught for nearly twenty years. While she was there, she took her final vows as a nun in 1937 and became known then as Mother Teresa, as was the custom of the Sisters of Loreto. In 1944, Mother Teresa became the school's principal.

During her time at St. Mary's, Mother Teresa became deeply aware of the poverty and suffering surrounding her in Calcutta. On September 10, 1946, she received what she later referred to as "a call within a call" to go to Calcutta's slums and work with the poorest of the poor. She finally received permission from her superiors to obey this call in 1948, so she left the Loreto convent and took up the dress that she made iconic: a simple white sari with a blue border. After six months of basic medical training, Mother Teresa turned to Calcutta's slums. Over time, she was joined by other volunteers, many of whom were students or former nuns from St. Mary's school. In 1950, Mother Teresa received official permission from the Vatican to form a new religious congregation, the Missionaries of

Charity (M.C.). At the time, there were twelve members. Mother Teresa remained the head of the Missionaries of Charity until shortly before her death.

Over the next several decades, the work of the Missionaries of Charity expanded rapidly. Mother Teresa and her fellow M.C.s founded hospices for the dying, leper houses, and orphanages throughout India. After the Missionaries of Charity were declared an International Religious Family in 1965, they spread to other countries, always caring for the poor, the unwanted, and the uncared for. Eventually, the order expanded to include the Missionaries of Charity Brothers (1963), contemplative branches of both Sisters and Brothers (1976 and 1979, respectively), and the Missionaries of Charity Fathers, a priestly branch (1984). The Sick and Suffering Co-Workers of the Missionaries of Charity was founded for lay Catholics and non-Catholics to support the work of M.C.s around the world. At the time of Mother Teresa's death, there were approximately four thousand M.C. sisters and three hundred M.C. brothers working in 610 missions in 123 countries.

Throughout her life of ministry, Mother Teresa made many humanitarian trips around the world, traveled to give speeches, and had many awards bestowed on her, including the Nobel Peace Prize in 1979.

After suffering from declining health and heart problems for several years, Mother Teresa died in Calcutta on September 5, 1997, at the age of 87. She was canonized as a saint of the Roman Catholic Church in 2016.

Suggested Reading

Murray, Paul. *I Loved Jesus in the Night: Teresa of Calcutta—A Secret Revealed.* Brewster, MA: Paraclete, 2008.

Teresa, Mother. *Come Be My Light: The Private Writings of the "Saint of Calcutta."* Edited by Brian Kolodiejchuk, M.C. New York: Image, 2007.

MARTIN LUTHER KING JR. (1929–1968)

The American civil rights leader Martin Luther King Jr. was born in Atlanta, Georgia, on January 15, 1929. He was given the name Michael at birth, but when he was a boy, his father changed his own name and that of his son to Martin Luther, in honor of the Protestant Reformer. King Jr.'s father was pastor of Atlanta's Ebenezer Baptist Church, a position he had taken over from his father-in-law. King grew up in a stable and loving family and was particularly distraught when his grandmother died in 1941, when he was twelve years old. Her death drove him to attempt suicide by jumping from his parents' second-story window.

King entered Morehouse College at age fifteen, in 1944, where he decided to enter the ministry. He went on to study at Crozer Theological Seminary, where he earned a bachelor's in divinity in 1951. He then attended Boston University and earned a doctorate in 1955, when he was twenty-six years old. In the midst of his doctoral studies, King met his wife, Coretta Scott, who was studying at the New England Conservatory of Music. They were married in 1953 and would go on to have four children.

While still working on his dissertation, King became pastor of Dexter Avenue Baptist Church in Montgomery, Alabama. In December of 1955, King helped lead the Montgomery bus boycott as the newly elected president of the Montgomery Improvement Association. During the boycott, which continued for over a year, King's home was bombed. After the Supreme Court ruled against Montgomery's bus segregation laws, King emerged as a formidable leader of the civil rights movement.

In 1957, King was part of the founding of the Southern Christian Leadership Conference (SCLC), an organization that coordinated and led civil rights efforts through nonviolent resistance and civil disobedience tactics. He was president of SCLC until his death. Under his leadership, SCLC engaged in advocacy throughout the United States, including efforts in Albany, Birmingham, Selma, and

Chicago. King traveled often to participate in civil rights demonstrations, give speeches, and provide support for the movement. He was arrested and assaulted multiple times. In the midst of it all, he found time to write five books. During a book signing for his first one, in 1958, King was stabbed by a Black woman who was later found unfit to stand trial by reason of insanity.

In 1960, King and his family moved to Atlanta, Georgia, where he became copastor with his father of Ebenezer Baptist Church, a role he held until his death.

In 1963, King led the protests in Birmingham, Alabama, where he penned his famous "Letter from Birmingham Jail." Later that year, he and other civil rights leaders organized the March on Washington, where he delivered his "I Have a Dream" speech. In 1964, he was named *Time*'s Man of the Year and was awarded the Nobel Peace Prize.

King received criticism for his speech at Riverside Church in 1967, in which he clearly opposed the Vietnam War. That same year, he was heavily involved with the planning of the Poor People's Campaign, which advocated for the rights of the poor of all races in the United States. While in Memphis, Tennessee, to support a sanitation workers' strike, King was assassinated on April 4, 1968.

Suggested Reading

King, Martin Luther, Jr. *I Have a Dream: Writings & Speeches That Changed the World.* Edited by James M. Washington. New York: Harper One, 1986.

Kunhardt, Peter, dir. *King in the Wilderness.* Pleasantville, NY: Kunhardt Films, 2018.

Oates, Stephen B. *Let the Trumpet Sound: A Life of Martin Luther King, Jr.* New York: Harper Perennial, 1982.

NOTES

INTRODUCTION: DEFINING THE DARKNESS

[1]American Psychiatric Association, *Diagnostic and Statistical Manual of Mental Disorders: DSM-5* (Arlington, VA: American Psychiatric Association, 2013).

[2]I am indebted here to Stanley W. Jackson, *Melancholia and Depression: From Hippocratic Times to Modern Times* (New Haven, CT: Yale University Press, 1986), 30-45.

[3]Jackson, *Melancholia and Depression*, 31-33; and Andrew Solomon, *The Noonday Demon: An Atlas of Depression* (New York: Scribner, 2001), 288-89.

[4]Solomon, *Noonday Demon*, 295-96, 299-301.

[5]Solomon, *Noonday Demon*, 293.

[6]Solomon, *Noonday Demon*, 292.

[7]Jackson, *Melancholia and Depression*, 66-67. One reason acedia was not considered synonymous with melancholy during this time period was that the cultural definition of melancholy then typically included delusions or hallucinations of some form.

[8]Solomon, *Noonday Demon*, 293.

[9]Solomon, *Noonday Demon*, 311.

[10]Solomon, *Noonday Demon*, 308-9.

1. MARTIN LUTHER

[1]Luther to Philip Melanchthon, Wartburg Castle, May 26, 1521, in *Luther's Correspondence and Other Contemporary Letters*, ed. and trans. Preserved Smith and Charles M. Jacobs (Philadelphia: Lutheran Publication Society, 1913), 2:35.

[2]Martin Luther, *Table Talk*, ed. and trans. William Hazlitt (London: Fount, 1995), 298-300, nos. 632, 633.

³Luther to Nicolaus von Amsdorf, Wartburg Castle, May 12, 1521, in Smith and Jacobs, *Luther's Correspondence,* 2:24.

⁴Luther to Philip Melanchthon, Wartburg Castle, May 12, 1521, in Smith and Jacobs, *Luther's Correspondence,* 2:23.

⁵Luther to George Spalatin, Wartburg Castle, September 19, 1521, in Smith and Jacobs, *Luther's Correspondence,* 2:57.

⁶Luther to Philip Melanchthon, Wartburg Castle, May 26, 1521, in Smith and Jacobs, *Luther's Correspondence,* 2:35.

⁷Quoted in Roland H. Bainton, *Here I Stand: A Life of Martin Luther* (Nashville: Abingdon Press, 1950), 30.

⁸Quoted in James M. Kittelson, *Luther the Reformer: The Story of the Man and His Career* (Minneapolis: Fortress Press, 1986), 79.

⁹Quoted in Eric W. Gritsch, *Martin—God's Court Jester: Luther in Retrospect* (Philadelphia: Fortress Press, 1983), 11.

¹⁰Luther's statement that he fought the devil with ink in Wartburg Castle has become the stuff of legend. Some think he physically threw his inkwell at the devil, splattering ink on the wall. Others interpret his words to mean the ink of his pen as he wrote.

¹¹One biographer, Richard Marius, claims Luther's productivity was a sign of his distressed mental state, describing him as "a man driven to superhuman labors by the demons of sorrow working within." Richard Marius, *Martin Luther: The Christian Between God and Death* (Cambridge, MA: Belknap Press, 1999), 276. Another theory is that Luther suffered from what we now call bipolar disorder and experienced dysphoric mania, which is simultaneous depressive and manic episodes. I find this argument compelling, but we do not have enough evidence and sit too far away to know for sure.

¹²In one place, Luther says, "All heaviness of mind and melancholy come of the devil. . . . Whosoever thou art, possessed with such heavy thoughts, know for certain, that they are a work of the devil." Luther, *Table Talk,* 300, no. 634. See also Luther, *Table Talk,* 288, no. 604.

¹³Luther, *Table Talk,* 282, no. 589.

¹⁴Some historians have traced the pattern of Luther's depression connected to his physical illnesses. See Gritsch, *Martin—God's Court Jester,* 147.

¹⁵Luther, *Table Talk,* 303-4, no. 645.

¹⁶Smith and Jacobs, *Luther's Correspondence,* 2:404-7.

¹⁷Smith and Jacobs, *Luther's Correspondence,* 2:407.

¹⁸Luther to Philip Melanchthon, August 2, 1527, in Smith and Jacobs, *Luther's Correspondence,* 2:409.

[19]Luther to John Agricola, August 21, 1527, in Smith and Jacobs, *Luther's Correspondence*, 2:412.

[20]Luther to Nicholas Hausmann, November 7, 1527, in Smith and Jacobs, *Luther's Correspondence*, 2:420.

[21]Luther to Philip Melanchthon, October 27, 1527, in Smith and Jacobs, *Luther's Correspondence*, 2:419.

[22]Luther, *Table Talk*, 29, 31, 291, and elsewhere.

[23]We do not know the precise date Luther wrote this hymn, but it was first published in 1529. It is not unreasonable to believe he wrote it during this dark season of life.

[24]Dorothea Wendebourg, "Selected Hymns," in *The Annotated Luther*, ed. Mary Jane Haemig (Minneapolis: Fortress Press, 2016), 4:133-34. The translation Wendebourg uses is that of George MacDonald and is more faithful to the original wording and style.

[25]See Kristen E. Kvam, "Consolation for Women Whose Pregnancies Have Not Gone Well, 1542," in *The Annotated Luther*, ed. Mary Jane Haemig, 4:421. This text was originally a brief afterword to a book written by one of Luther's friends. By the time he wrote it, Luther's wife had already suffered at least one miscarriage, and they had lost an eight-month-old daughter, Elisabeth, in 1528. It's clear the grief suffered by parents is a concern to Luther.

[26]Martin Luther, *Letters of Spiritual Counsel*, ed. and trans. Theodore G. Tappert (Philadelphia: Westminster Press, 1955), 51.

[27]Luther, *Letters of Spiritual Counsel*, 51.

[28]Quoted in Gritsch, *Martin—God's Court Jester*, 83.

[29]Quoted in Gritsch, *Martin—God's Court Jester*, 83.

[30]Quoted in Gritsch, *Martin—God's Court Jester*, 87.

[31]Luther to Jerome Weller, July 1530, in *Letters of Spiritual Counsel*, 85-87.

[32]Luther, *Letters of Spiritual Counsel*, 95.

[33]Luther to Mrs. Jonas von Stockhausen, November 27, 1532, in *Letters of Spiritual Counsel*, 91. On the same day Luther wrote this letter, he also sent one to his friend Jonas ("the husband" in this letter) with advice for his depression, offering separate advice for his depressed friend and the wife who cared for him.

[34]Luther, *Table Talk*, 306, no. 654.

[35]Luther to Jonas Von Stockhausen, November 27, 1532, in *Letters of Spiritual Counsel*, 89.

[36]Luther to Matthias Weller, October 7, 1534, in *Letters of Spiritual Counsel*, 96.

[37]Quoted in Rudolf K. Markwald and Marilynn Morris Markwald, *Katharina Von Bora: A Reformation Life* (Saint Louis: Concordia, 2002), 139-40.

[38]Luther to Prince Joachim of Anhalt, May 23, 1534, in response to reports that he was both ill and depressed, in *Letters of Spiritual Counsel*, 93.

2. HANNAH ALLEN

[1]Hannah Allen, *[Satan, his Methods and Malice baffled:] A Narrative of God's gracious dealings with that Christian Mrs. Hannah Allen . . .* (London: John Wallis, 1683), 8, 10.

[2]Allen, *Narrative of God's Gracious Dealings*, 17.

[3]Allen, *Narrative of God's Gracious Dealings*, 18.

[4]Allen, *Narrative of God's Gracious Dealings*, 20.

[5]The phrase "religious melancholy" was introduced by Robert Burton in his monumental *Anatomy of Melancholy*, which was first published in 1621. For an overview of the history of religious melancholy and many other examples of people who suffered from it, see Julius H. Rubin, *Religious Melancholy and the Protestant Experience in America* (New York: Oxford University Press, 1994).

[6]Allen, *Narrative of God's Gracious Dealings*, 21.

[7]Allen, *Narrative of God's Gracious Dealings*, 40.

[8]Allen, *Narrative of God's Gracious Dealings*, 42-43.

[9]Allen, *Narrative of God's Gracious Dealings*, 48.

[10]Allen, *Narrative of God's Gracious Dealings*, 55, italics original.

[11]This sermon can be accessed for free online. I'd encourage you to read it, as it still has helpful insights and practical suggestions for those struggling with depression today.

[12]Allen, *Narrative of God's Gracious Dealings*, 26.

[13]Allen, *Narrative of God's Gracious Dealings*, 28.

[14]Richard Baxter, *Preservatives Against Melancholy and Overmuch Sorrow. Or the Cure of both by Faith and Physick* (London: W.R., 1713), 16.

[15]Allen, *Narrative of God's Gracious Dealings*, 33-34.

[16]Allen, *Narrative of God's Gracious Dealings*, 46.

[17]Self-starvation or "religious anorexia" is another feature of religious melancholy that is mentioned by Baxter, in the seventeenth century, and Rubin as a modern historian. I first discovered Hannah Allen in a book about the history of psychiatry in relation to eating disorders.

[18]Allen, *Narrative of God's Gracious Dealings*, 58.

[19]Allen, *Narrative of God's Gracious Dealings*, 64-65. This was in the winter of 1665–1666. Hannah says that in the spring she began to eat a little better, though she doesn't say why.

[20]Allen, *Narrative of God's Gracious Dealings*, 62.

[21]Allen, *Narrative of God's Gracious Dealings*, 60.

[22]Allen, *Narrative of God's Gracious Dealings*, 68-69.

[23]Allen, *Narrative of God's Gracious Dealings*, 72.

[24]Allen, *Narrative of God's Gracious Dealings*, i.

3. DAVID BRAINERD

[1]*The Life and Diary of David Brainerd*, ed. Jonathan Edwards (Middletown, DE: ReadaClassic, 2010), 65.

[2]*Life and Diary of David Brainerd*, 6. Unfortunately, Edwards removed large chunks of Brainerd's diary—including many in which Brainerd talks about his depression—and inserted his own summaries of the passages he omitted. The original diaries were destroyed by a descendant, so we'll never know Brainerd's original words for these passages. So bear in mind that what remains could not be escaped, even with Edwards's editorial scissors.

[3]*Life and Diary of David Brainerd*, 67.

[4]*Life and Diary of David Brainerd*, 30.

[5]Brainerd was only one of many who were fined, expelled, or threatened with losing their degree during this tumultuous period of Clap's tenure.

[6]We will never know the full extent of Brainerd's thoughts in and about this season of his life, both because he destroyed his college diaries and because of Edwards's censorship to not lay excessive blame at the feet of the Yale authorities.

One of Brainerd's descendants, Thomas Brainerd, did have access to a diary now lost to us, which included David's account of his expulsion. He paints a severe picture of the effects of the expulsion on David's mental and emotional state—one with much more outrage than we find in Edwards's version. Thomas quotes Brainerd as comparing the college authorities to "the Holy Court of Inquisition," torturing students like him while insisting it's for their spiritual benefit. He even goes so far as to say there is "no doubt that the life of David Brainerd was shortened by his college persecution." Quoted in Jonathan Edwards, *The Works of Jonathan Edwards*, ed. Perry Miller, vol. 7, *The Life of David Brainerd*, ed. Norman Pettit (New Haven, CT: Yale University Press, 1985), 44-45.

[7]After Brainerd wrote a lengthy apology to the college board, and under the influence of Brainerd's friends, Clap did eventually allow for him to receive his degree but only under the condition that he complete one more year of study at Yale. Brainerd did not want to return to the school; he simply wanted his degree, and he thought that the further study and ministry experience he had gained since his expulsion would be sufficient to make up for the years he missed. He insisted on being allowed to graduate with his degree with his original class.

When Clap refused to comply with this desire, it was Brainerd, and not Clap, who in the end refused reinstatement.

[8]Brainerd to John Brainerd, April 30, 1743, in *The Diary and Journal of David Brainerd* (London: Andrew Melrose, 1902), 2:270-71, italics original.

[9]Brainerd first showed signs of tuberculosis while he was a student at Yale, when he began spitting up blood in the summer of 1740. This was three years before the beginning of his ministry at Kaunaumeek in April 1743, and seven years before his death in October 1747. He battled tuberculosis and its degrading health effects his entire missionary and preaching career.

[10]*Life and Diary of David Brainerd*, 72.

[11]*Diary and Journal of David Brainerd*, 2:273.

[12]*Life and Diary of David Brainerd*, 90.

[13]*Life and Diary of David Brainerd*, 171-73. For further explanation of the reactions and attitudes of the colonists, see John A. Grigg, *The Lives of David Brainerd: The Making of an American Evangelical Icon* (New York: Oxford University Press, 2009), 103-7.

[14]*Life and Diary of David Brainerd*, 111.

[15]*Life and Diary of David Brainerd*, 111.

[16]*Life and Diary of David Brainerd*, 112.

[17]*Life and Diary of David Brainerd*, 112.

[18]*Life and Diary of David Brainerd*, 48.

[19]Edwards, *Works*, 7:35.

[20]Quoted in Grigg, *Lives of David Brainerd*, 33. This was the advice given to him by Phineas Fiske, whom he lived with in preparation for college at Yale.

[21]*Life and Diary of David Brainerd*, 85.

[22]*Life and Diary of David Brainerd*, 112.

[23]*Life and Diary of David Brainerd*, 113.

[24]*Life and Diary of David Brainerd*, 60.

[25]*Life and Diary of David Brainerd*, 37.

[26]*Life and Diary of David Brainerd*, 126.

[27]*Life and Diary of David Brainerd*, 133.

[28]*Life and Diary of David Brainerd*, 136.

[29]*Life and Diary of David Brainerd*, 117.

[30]*Life and Diary of David Brainerd*, 144.

[31]*Life and Diary of David Brainerd*, 114-15. In his journal, he wrote, "At this time I was affected with a sense of the important trust committed to me; yet was composed, and solemn, without distraction: and I hope that then, as many times before, I gave myself up to God, to be for him, and not for another. O that I

might always be engaged in the service of God, and duly remember the solemn charge I have received, in the presence of God, angels, and men. Amen. May I be assisted of God for this purpose."

[32]*Diary and Journal of David Brainerd*, 2:8, 2:214. We know a little of Tatamy's history from outside sources. Before working with Brainerd, he had been employed as a translator for William Penn's government. Brainerd, in his public journal, lists his name as Moses Tinda Tautamy, fifty years old. He says he employed him July 1744.

[33]*Diary and Journal of David Brainerd*, 2:8-9, 2:214. He would tell Brainerd repeatedly, "It signifies nothing for us to try, they will never turn."

[34]"He now addressed the Indians with admirable fervency, and scarcely knew when to leave off. Sometimes when I had concluded my discourse, and was returning homeward, he would tarry behind to repeat and inculcate what had been spoken. . . . He has likewise of late had more satisfaction respecting his own state, has been much enlivened and assisted in his work, and been a great comfort to me." *Diary and Journal of David Brainerd*, 2:14.

[35]When Brainerd arrived, he preached to the women he found, completely unaware of their culture that, according to historian John Grigg, gave Lenni Lenape women a role in passing on and preserving spiritual practices and experiences for their families. He had no idea of the weight their words would have when they traveled up to fifteen miles to tell their kinsmen to come hear the message of this White religious man. Brainerd simply saw his audience increasing. See Grigg, *Lives of David Brainerd*, 89-90.

[36]*Diary and Journal of David Brainerd*, 2:19. He says, "It was surprising to see how their hearts seemed to be pierced with the tender and melting invitations of the Gospel, when there was not a word of terror spoken to them."

[37]*Diary and Journal of David Brainerd*, 2:28-29. Brainerd patterns his description of the response of his Native community at Crossweeksung after the expected typical conversion experience of the day and portrays a similar scene to what Jonathan Edwards had described in *A Faithful Narrative* about his congregation in Northampton. Individuals are falling under conviction of sin, troubled and concerned over the state of their soul, then moving through this distress to a sense of comfort in the sheer grace of God. It is important not to miss this moment. He is saying that the powerful work of God and the free gift of his grace is just as much for Edwards's White community as it is for his precious people in New Jersey. In fact, when some White settlers appear to observe Brainerd's services, he calls them "careless spectators" and "white heathen,"

while it is his Native congregation who is most receptive to and transformed by God's Word.

[38]*Diary and Journal of David Brainerd*, 2:22.

[39]*Diary and Journal of David Brainerd*, 2:62-63.

[40]The legend of the romance of David Brainerd and Jerusha Edwards arose in the nineteenth century, long after both of their deaths. We don't have substantial evidence to prove an engagement or love between them. We do know Jerusha was his caretaker and accompanied him on his final trip to Boston. We also know they were buried together, but this was in the Edwards's family plot, so there is nothing particularly notable there. The legend seems to have arisen from one quote we have from Brainerd's sick bed: "He looked on her [Jerusha] very pleasantly, and said, 'Dear Jerusha, are you willing to part with me?—I am quite willing to part with you: I am willing to part with all my friends: I am willing to part with my dear brother John, although I love him the best of any creature living: I have committed him and all my friends to God and can leave them to God. Though, if I thought I should not see you and be happy with you in another world, I could not bear to part with you. But we shall spend a happy eternity together!'" *Life and Diary of David Brainerd*, 244.

[41]*Life and Diary of David Brainerd*, 236.

[42]*Life and Diary of David Brainerd*, 245-46.

[43]*Life and Diary of David Brainerd*, 139.

[44]*Life and Diary of David Brainerd*, 139.

[45]Quoted in David Wynbeek, *David Brainerd: Beloved Yankee* (Grand Rapids, MI: Eerdmans, 1961), 236.

[46]Though this may be the case, we cannot underestimate the impact Brainerd had on those who did come to faith. There are reports from the nineteenth century of Native Christians who traced their spiritual heritage back to Brainerd, and there is still a Christian presence in the Lenni Lenape community today.

[47]Edwards edited and published *The Life and Diary* during a controversy with his church, in which he wanted to institute stricter rules for who could be considered a member of the church and would be allowed to partake of Communion. He released Brainerd's diary at a particular time and for a particular purpose, and many (including, it seems, his congregation at the time, considering he was fired shortly after its publication) believe it to be a message from Edwards, holding up David Brainerd as the ideal picture of Christian spirituality. Apparently he wanted each Christian in his parish to live up to the standards of Brainerd in order to be considered fully converted. Thus, consciously or subconsciously, the words of Brainerd that Edwards chose to cut or

reword, to emphasize or to leave untouched, were serving to present a particular picture of Christian spirituality.

[48]See Grigg, *Lives of Brainerd*, 147-54. Like Edwards, Wesley took significant editorial liberties to craft Brainerd into an appropriate figurehead for his movement.

[49]Quoted in Grigg, *Lives of David Brainerd*, 178.

[50]Edwards, *Works*, 7:509.

4. WILLIAM COWPER

[1]*Memoir of the Early Life of William Cowper, Esq.* (Philadelphia: Edward Earle, 1816), 27-28.

[2]Cowper wrote his poignant poem "On the Receipt of My Mother's Picture" after receiving a copy of her portrait from a relative. Poetic words of his childhood sorrow and his treasured memories of her loving presence came vividly to the page more than fifty years after her death.

We also know of the lasting impact of her loss from a sympathy note Cowper wrote to a friend who had recently lost his mother. He said, "While I live, I must regret a comfort of which I was deprived so early. I can truly say, that not a week passes (perhaps I might with equal veracity say a day) in which I do not think of her. Such was the impression her tenderness made upon me, though the opportunity she had for showing it was so short." William Cowper to Joseph Hill, November 1784, in *The Works of Cowper and Thomson* (Philadelphia: J. Grigg, 1831), 268.

[3]*Memoir of the Early Life*, 32.

[4]*Memoir of the Early Life*, 34.

[5]In his poetry, Cowper referred to Theodora as "Delia."

[6]A slip from Lady Hesketh (who was Theodora's sister, Harriet) informed Cowper that she knew Anonymous's identity. Though he never found out his secret patron, he knew Lady Hesketh was in contact with him/her, and he appointed her a surrogate "thanks-receiver general."

[7]Charles Ryskamp, *William Cowper of the Inner Temple, Esq.: A Study of His Life and Works to the Year 1768* (Cambridge, UK: Cambridge University Press, 1959), 106. Written in 1757, after William Russell's death.

[8]From a poem written to law-school friend Robert Lloyd while an undergrad. This is one of Cowper's earliest existing poems, 1754:

> That, with a black, infernal train,
> Make cruel inroads on my brain,
> And daily threaten to drive thence

My little garrison of sense;
The fierce banditti which I mean
Are gloomy thoughts, led on by spleen.

Quoted in Thomas Wright, *The Life of William Cowper* (London: T. Fisher Unwin, 1892), 67.

[9]This would not be the first time Cowper found himself in financial need. He was notoriously bad with money and throughout his life came to depend on the financial generosity of his friends.

[10]*Memoir of the Early Life*, 44.

[11]*Memoir of the Early Life*, 45.

[12]See *Memoir of the Early Life*, 46.

[13]*Memoir of the Early Life*, 52-53.

[14]Quoted in Ryskamp, *William Cowper of the Inner Temple*, 109. This was written during his last year at the Inner Temple.

[15]*Memoir of the Early Life*, 87-88. "A strange and horrible darkness fell upon me. If it were possible, that a heavy blow could light on the brain, without touching the skull, such was the sensation I felt. I clapped my hand to my forehead, and cried aloud, through the pain it gave me. At every stroke, my thoughts and expressions became more wild and incoherent; all that remained clear was the sense of sin, and the expectation of punishment."

[16]*Memoir of the Early Life*, 90.

[17]*Memoir of the Early Life*, 92.

[18]*Memoir of the Early Life*, 93.

[19]Though we'll never know for sure, it's quite possible this Bible was opened to this passage and strategically placed in Cowper's path by Dr. Cotton.

[20]*Memoir of the Early Life*, 97.

[21]*Memoir of the Early Life*, 99.

[22]Cowper to Lady Hesketh, Huntingdon, July 1, 1765, in *Works of Cowper and Thomson*, 165.

[23]Wright, *Life of William Cowper*, 128.

[24]Cowper to John Newton, July 27, 1783, in *Works of Cowper and Thomson*, 234-35.

[25]William Cowper to Lady Hesketh, January 16, 1786, in *The Selected Letters of William Cowper*, ed. Mark Van Doren (New York: Farrar, Straus, and Young, Inc., 1951), 176.

[26]Newton said, "Mr. Cowper is still in the depths. Sometimes I have hope that his deliverance is at hand; at others I am almost at a stand." Quoted in Wright, *Life of William Cowper*, 212-13. John and Mary Newton and Mrs. Unwin remind us

that caring for those who are depressed can be a challenge. It is not an easy task, and it does weigh on the caretakers. Newton admits that sometimes he found Cowper's unexpected, extended stay in his condition "inconvenient and trying" (quoted in Wright, *Life of William Cowper*, 213). But they all willingly cared for him with grace. They give us a picture of the beauty that comes in steady love for a hurting friend. With much prayer—and real sacrifice—they bore the weight of caring for someone who could give them little in return.

[27]Quoted in Wright, *Life of William Cowper,* 213-14.

[28]Cowper to John Newton, January 1784, in *Selected Letters*, 129-31.

[29]Cowper, *Selected Letters*, 129-31. Cowper continued his letter: "The latter end of next month will complete a period of eleven years in which I have spoken no other language. It is a long time for a man, whose eyes were once opened, to spend in darkness; long enough to make despair an inveterate habit; and such it is in me. My friends, I know, expect that I shall see yet again. They think it necessary to the existence of divine truth, that he who once had possession of it should never finally lose it. I admit the solidity of this reasoning in every case but my own."

[30]Cowper, *Selected Letters*, 129-31.

[31]Cowper to John Newton, February 19, 1788, in *Selected Letters*, 240-41.

[32]Quoted in George B. Cheever, *Lectures on the Life, Genius, and Insanity of Cowper* (New York: Robert Carter & Brothers, 1856), 329.

[33]Cowper to John Newton, February 5, 1790, in *Selected Letters*, 248-49.

[34]Wright, *Life of William Cowper*, 481-84.

[35]Cowper to William Unwin, April 6, 1780, in *Works of Cowper and Thomson*, 187.

[36]Though passionate about his hobbies, Cowper moved from one activity to another frequently. "So long as I am pleased with an employment," he wrote, "I am capable of unwearied application, because my feelings are all of the intense kind. I never received a *little* pleasure from any thing in my life; if I am delighted, it is in the extreme. The unhappy consequence of this temperature is, that my attachment to any occupation seldom outlives the novelty of it." Cowper to William Unwin, May 8, 1780, in *Works of Cowper and Thomson*, 189.

[37]Cowper to William Unwin, November 10, 1783, in *Works of Cowper and Thomson*, 241. It seems Cowper's friend William Unwin also occasionally struggled with depression. Sometimes Cowper offered advice to him in his letters, including encouraging him to exercise: "I have observed in your two last letters somewhat of a dejection and melancholy, that I am afraid you do not sufficiently strive against. I suspect you of being too sedentary. 'You can not walk.' Why you can not is best known to yourself. I am sure your legs are long enough, and your

person does not overload them. But I beseech you ride, and ride often. I think I have heard you say, you can not even do that without an object. Is not health an object? Assure yourself that easy chairs are no friends to cheerfulness, and that a long winter spent by the fireside is a prelude to an unhealthy spring."

[38]"I find constant employment necessary, and therefore take care to be constantly employed. Manual occupations do not engage the mind sufficiently, as I know by experience having tried many. But composition, especially of verse, absorbs it wholly." Cowper, *Works of Cowper and Thomson*, 278.

[39]Cowper to Lady Hesketh, January 16, 1786, in *Selected Letters*, 175.

[40]Quoted in Wright, *Life of William Cowper*, 535.

[41]Ryskamp, *Cowper of the Inner Temple*, 101.

[42]Cowper to William Unwin, November 18, 1782, in *Works of Cowper and Thomson*, 228.

[43]Wright, *Life of William Cowper*, 593.

[44]Quoted in Wright, *Life of William Cowper*, 593.

[45]Cowper, *Selected Letters*, 277-78.

[46]Lady Hesketh was the first of Cowper's relatives to realize just how poor his and Mrs. Unwin's health had become. She visited them and then stayed through most of 1794, before they moved in with Cousin Johnson. During her visit, she wrote Johnson a vivid letter of Cowper's condition: "He now does nothing but walk incessantly backwards and forwards, either in his study or in his bed-chamber. He really does not sometimes sit down for more than half an hour the whole day, except at meal-times, when, as I said before, he takes hardly anything. He has left off bathing his feet, will take no laudanum, and lives in a constant state of terror that is dreadful to behold! He is now come to expect daily, and even hourly, that he shall be carried away; and kept in his room from the time breakfast was over till four o'clock on Sunday last, in spite of repeated messages from Madam, because he was afraid somebody would take possession of his bed, and prevent his lying down on it any more!" Letter dated May 5, 1795, quoted in Wright, *Life of William Cowper*, 632-33.

[47]See Wright, *Life of William Cowper*, 651.

[48]Cowper to Lady Hesketh, January 22, 1796, in *Selected Letters*, 298.

[49]Wright, *Life of William Cowper*, 648.

[50]Cowper to Lady Hesketh, June 1, 1798, in *Selected Letters*, 301.

[51]William Cowper, *The Complete Poetical Works of William Cowper, Esq., Including the Hymns and Translations from Madame Guion, Milton, etc. With a Memoir of the Author by Rev. H. Stebbing, A.M.* (New York: D. Appleton & Co., 1869), 498-99.

[52]Cowper to William Unwin, August 27, 1785, in *Works of Cowper and Thomson*, 276.

[53]M. Seeley, *The Later Evangelical Fathers* (London: Seeley, Jackson, & Halliday, 1879), 115.

5. CHARLES SPURGEON

[1]*The Autobiography of Charles H. Spurgeon*, ed. Susannah Spurgeon and W. J. Harrald, vol. 2, *1854-1860* (Philadelphia: American Baptist Publication Society, 1899), 2:205-6. This story is dramatized from the account given in Spurgeon's autobiography.

[2]*Autobiography of Charles H. Spurgeon*, 2:38.

[3]*Autobiography of Charles H. Spurgeon*, 2:50.

[4]*Autobiography of Charles H. Spurgeon*, 2:44.

[5]*Autobiography of Charles H. Spurgeon*, 2:195-96.

[6]William Williams, *Personal Reminiscences of Charles Haddon Spurgeon*, 2nd ed. (London: Religious Tract Society, 1895), 166.

[7]*Autobiography of Charles H. Spurgeon*, 2:192.

[8]Charles Spurgeon, "The Exaltation of Christ," in *The New Park Street Pulpit* (Pasadena, TX: Pilgrim Publications, 1981), 2:378. When Spurgeon returned to his congregation on Nov. 2, 1856, after nearly a month away, he preached on Philippians 2:9-11, the same verses that had come to him in the garden: "In the midst of calamities . . . the great question which [the Christian] asks himself, and asks of others too, is this—Is Christ's kingdom safe? . . . he finds it sufficient consolation, in the midst of all the breaking in pieces which he endures, to think that Christ's throne stands fast and firm, and that though the earth hath rocked beneath *his* feet, yet Christ standeth on a rock which never can be moved."

[9]In his *Autobiography* (2:193) Susannah would say Spurgeon "carried the scars of that conflict to his dying day."

[10]*Autobiography of Charles H. Spurgeon*, 2:220.

[11]Eric W. Hayden, *Searchlight on Spurgeon: Spurgeon Speaks for Himself* (Pasadena, TX: Pilgrim Publications, 1973), 162.

[12]Charles Spurgeon, "Our Leader Through the Darkness," in *Metropolitan Tabernacle Pulpit*, vol. 59, sermon 3370, accessed August 1, 2017, www.spurgeongems .org/vols58-60/chs3370.pdf.

[13]*Autobiography of Charles H. Spurgeon*, vol. 3, *1856-1878*, 3:243-45. During this particular illness, he suffered six weeks of "pain and weakness" and spent twelve Sabbaths away from the pulpit.

[14]*Autobiography of Charles H. Spurgeon*, 3:183.

[15]In his *Autobiography*, vol. 4, *1878-1892*, (4:253), Spurgeon had this to say: "Just now, the Lord Jesus is betrayed by not a few of His professed ministers. He is being crucified afresh in the perpetual attacks of scepticism against His blessed gospel; and it may be that things will wax worse and worse." Although he didn't like the controversy, he felt he was simply following orders: "Controversy is never a very happy element for the child of God: he would far rather be in communion with his Lord than be engaged in defending the faith, or in attacking error. But the soldier of Christ knows no choice in his Master's commands."

[16]*Autobiography of Charles H. Spurgeon*, 4:255.

[17]Spurgeon to a friend, February 15, 1888, in *Letters of Charles Haddon Spurgeon*, ed. Iain H. Murray (Edinburgh: Banner of Truth Trust, 1992), 186.

[18]*Autobiography of Charles H. Spurgeon*, 4:255.

[19]See *Autobiography of Charles H. Spurgeon*, 4:255. His wife, Susannah, says it was evident to all those close to him that "his fight for the faith had cost him his life."

[20]Charles Spurgeon, "A Frail Leaf," in *Metropolitan Tabernacle Pulpit*, vol. 57, sermon 3269, accessed August 31, 2017, www.spurgeongems.org/vols55-57/chs3269.pdf.

[21]Charles Spurgeon, *The Treasury of David* (Grand Rapids, MI: Zondervan, 1957), 4:3. Spurgeon's exposition of Psalm 88 here seems full of autobiographical descriptions of the darkness and depths of depression.

[22]Charles Spurgeon, "The Minister's Fainting Fits," in *Lectures to My Students* (Albany, OR: Ages Digital Library, 1996), 180-81.

[23]For example, "Some strong-minded people are very apt to be hard upon nervous folk, and to say, 'They should not get into that state.' And we are liable to speak harshly to people who are very depressed in spirit, and say to them, 'Really, you ought to rouse yourself out of such a state.' I hope none of you will ever have such an experience of this depression of spirit as I have had; yet I have learned from it to be very tender with all fellow sufferers. The Lord have mercy on them." Charles Spurgeon, "The Saddest Cry from the Cross," in *Metropolitan Tabernacle Pulpit*, vol. 48, sermon 2803, accessed July 28, 2017, www.spurgeongems.org /vols46-48/chs2803.pdf.

[24]Charles Spurgeon, "A Song and a Solace," in *Metropolitan Tabernacle Pulpit*, vol. 46, sermon 2682, accessed July 28, 2017, www.spurgeongems.org/vols46-48 /chs2682.pdf.

[25]Charles Spurgeon, "Sweet Stimulants for the Fainting Soul," in *Metropolitan Tabernacle Pulpit*, vol. 48, sermon 2798, accessed August 31, 2017, www.spurgeongems .org/vols46-48/chs2798.pdf.

[26]Spurgeon, "Minister's Fainting Fits," 182.

[27]Spurgeon, "Minister's Fainting Fits," 182.

[28]Charles Spurgeon, "Elijah Fainting," in *Metropolitan Tabernacle Pulpit*, vol. 47, sermon 2725, accessed August 31, 2017, www.spurgeongems.org/vols46 -48/chs2725.pdf.

[29]Charles Spurgeon, "The Shank-Bone Sermon—or, True Believers and Their Helpers," in *Metropolitan Tabernacle Pulpit*, vol. 36, sermon 2138, accessed July 28, 2017, www.spurgeongems.org/vols34-36/chs2138.pdf.

[30]Spurgeon, "Shank-Bone Sermon."

[31]Charles Spurgeon, preface to *Faith's Checkbook* (Chicago: Moody Press, 1993), ii-iii.

[32]Charles Spurgeon, "The Roaring Lion," in *Metropolitan Tabernacle Pulpit*, vol. 7, sermon 419, accessed August 31, 2017, www.spurgeongems.org/vols7-9/chs419.pdf.

[33]Spurgeon, *Faith's Checkbook*, 133.

[34]Spurgeon, "Elijah Fainting."

[35]Williams, *Personal Reminiscences*, 177.

6. Mother Teresa

[1]The words throughout this scene are quotations or paraphrases of Mother Teresa's actual thoughts and prayers, as quoted in Mother Teresa, *Come Be My Light: The Private Writings of the "Saint of Calcutta,"* ed. Brian Kolodiejchuk, M.C. (New York: Image, 2007).

[2]Some may wonder why Teresa of Calcutta bears the name "Mother." She was first called Mother Teresa, or rather Mother Mary Teresa, while a part of the Sisters of Loreto, where all sisters bore the name "Mother." When she left that order to form the Missionaries of Charity, she was merely "Mary Teresa," but then regained the title "Mother" when she became the elected Mother Superior of the congregation. She so embodied the love of a "mother" that many came to simply refer to her as this, even those outside of her religious congregation.

[3]Mother Teresa, *Come Be My Light*, 121.

[4]By the time of Mother Teresa's death in 1997, the Missionaries of Charity claimed approximately four thousand members and 610 foundations in 123 countries.

[5]Mother Teresa, *Come Be My Light*, 186-87. This is part of a prayer enclosed with a letter to Father Picachy dated July 3, 1959. She felt God wanted her to reveal everything to him about her interior state.

[6]During the process of her canonization, private letters to a handful of her confessors and spiritual superiors were published in the book *Come Be My Light*. It revealed the true state of Mother Teresa's soul to the world—and to some of those who had worked with her closely for decades. If you want to know more about her experience, I highly recommend this book to you.

[7]Mother Teresa, *Come Be My Light*, 221.

[8]Mother Teresa, *Come Be My Light*, 226.

[9]Mother Teresa, *Come Be My Light*, 161.

[10]Mother Teresa to Father Neuner, 1961, in *Come Be My Light*, 210-11. He gave a retreat for the Missionaries of Charity, and she confided in him. He asked her to write down her experiences.

[11]Mother Teresa, *Come Be My Light*, 210.

[12]Mother Teresa to Archbishop Perier, September 1959, in *Come Be My Light*, 191.

[13]Mother Teresa to Archbishop Perier, December 15, 1955, in *Come Be My Light*, 163.

[14]Mother Teresa to Father Neuner, before January 8, 1965, in *Come Be My Light*, 250.

[15]Mother Teresa to Father Neuner, May 12, 1962, in *Come Be My Light*, 232. The letter continues in such a way that describes her extreme surrender to God's will, even at the expense of her own pain: "And yet this terrible pain has never made me desire to have it different.—What's more, I want it to be like this for as long as He wants it."

[16]Mother Teresa, *Come Be My Light*, 214.

7. MARTIN LUTHER KING JR.

[1]This story is recounted in Taylor Branch, *At Canaan's Edge: America in the King Years, 1965-68* (New York: Simon & Schuster, 2006), 708, and elsewhere.

[2]*The Autobiography of Martin Luther King, Jr.*, ed. Clayborne Carson (New York: Warner Books, 1998), 58.

[3]*Autobiography of Martin Luther King, Jr.*, 71.

[4]He told his congregation at Dexter in the year after the bus boycotts that he often prayed for God to help him see himself in the right perspective. See his sermon "Conquering Self-Centeredness" given at Dexter on August 11, 1957, in *The Papers of Martin Luther King, Jr.*, ed. Clayborne Carson (Berkeley: University of California Press, 2000), 4:255.

[5]*King in the Wilderness*, directed by Peter Kunhardt (Pleasantville, NY: Kunhardt Films, 2018).

[6]If you find you do not know much about the civil rights movement or Dr. King's role in it, I would encourage you to learn more about this important man and movement. The one-volume biography *Let the Trumpet Sound* by Stephen B. Oates (New York: Harper Perennial, 1982) is an excellent resource for an overview of King's work.

[7]I mention SCLC because of King's critical involvement, but there were many other important organizations and leaders during this time period, who should not be overlooked at King's expense.

[8]My thanks go to Josina Guess for recommending the book *Black Pain: It Just Looks Like We're Not Hurting* by Terrie M. Williams for a vivid portrayal of the challenges related to depression within the Black community. I commend this book to you.

[9]See Clarence Jones's interview in *King in the Wilderness*.

[10]In March 1968, after violence erupted at a march in Memphis, King said to Ralph Abernathy and Bernard Lee, "Maybe we just have to admit that the day of violence is here. . . . And maybe we just have to give up and let violence take its course." King put on a brave and confident face for the press the following day, insisting on the contagious nature of nonviolence, but in private, he still wondered if his influence was at its end. To his friend Stanley Levison he said, "You know, their point is, 'Martin Luther King is dead, he's finished. . . . His nonviolence is nothing. No one is listening to it.'" Branch, *At Canaan's Edge*, 734, 738-39.

[11]"The average man reaches this point maybe in his late forties or early fifties. But when you reach it so young, your life becomes a kind of decrescendo. . . . A man who hits the peak at twenty-seven has a tough job ahead. People will be expecting me to pull rabbits out of the hat for the rest of my life. If I don't or there are no rabbits to be pulled, then they'll say I'm no good." Quoted in *Autobiography of Martin Luther King, Jr.*, 106, from the *New York Post*, April 14, 1957.

[12]One local Black Chicago pastor, when asked by a reporter what he would suggest King do, said, "I would suggest that when it comes to our city, he should get the hell outta here." In *King in the Wilderness*.

[13]*King in the Wilderness*.

[14]At one point, J. Edgar Hoover and his minions went so far as to send King a tape with recordings suggesting his marital indiscretions along with a note suggesting he commit suicide and remove himself from public disgrace. See Oates, *Let the Trumpet Sound*, 331, and elsewhere.

[15]Joseph Rosenbloom, *Redemption: Martin Luther King Jr.'s Last 31 Hours* (Boston: Beacon Press, 2018), 82.

[16]Branch, *At Canaan's Edge*, 216. The pills had stopped working by April 1965.

[17]Rosenbloom, *Redemption*, 82.

[18]*King in the Wilderness*.

[19]Perhaps one of the sweetest notes King received was from a young girl as he convalesced after the stabbing. She told him simply, "I'm so glad you didn't sneeze." It's obvious her words stuck with him. He quoted them during his last speech in Memphis the night before his assassination.

[20]Rosenbloom, *Redemption*, 109, 112. "He said that the choice for humankind was no longer between violence and nonviolence. Tapping his fingers on the rostrum, he said the choice, rather, was between nonviolence and 'nonexistence.'"

[21]Martin Luther King Jr., *I Have a Dream: Writings & Speeches That Changed the World*, ed. James M. Washington (New York: Harper One, 1986), 203.

[22]Rosenbloom, *Redemption*, 114.

[23]Rosenbloom, *Redemption*, 114.

[24]Rosenbloom, *Redemption*, 115.

[25]This biographer, ironically, notes the importance of humor and laughter as coping mechanisms for Black Americans, beginning in the days of slavery. Humor did not mean that life was free of hurt. It merely gave the Black community a way to find hope in the midst of it. He includes this footnote: "[James Weldon] Johnson would later admit that 'I have since learned that this ability to laugh heartily is, in part, the salvation of the American Negro. . . .' Black thinkers such as Claude McKay and W. E. B. DuBois offered similar insights while acknowledging that the ability to laugh in the face of oppression was perhaps their people's greatest gift from God." Lewis V. Baldwin, *Behind the Public Veil: The Humanness of Martin Luther King Jr.* (Minneapolis: Fortress Press, 2016), 261-62.

[26]*King in the Wilderness.*

[27]King said, "With this music, a rich heritage from our ancestors who had the stamina and the moral fiber to be able to find beauty in broken fragments of music . . . we can articulate our deepest groans and passionate yearnings—and end always on a note of hope that God is going to help us work it out. . . . Through this music, the Negro is able to dip down into wells of a deeply pessimistic situation and danger-fraught circumstances and to bring forth a marvelous, sparkling, fluid optimism. He knows it is still dark in his world, but somehow, he finds a ray of light." *Autobiography of Martin Luther King, Jr.*, 178. For more on the importance and role of the spirituals within the Black community, see James Cone's book *The Spirituals and the Blues: An Interpretation* (New York: Seabury Press, 1972).

[28]James Cone specifically mentions this song in his book and explains one reason why it may have been so encouraging to King: "Whites may suppress black history and define Africans as savages, but the words of slave masters do not have to be taken seriously when the oppressed know that they have a *somebodiness* that is guaranteed by the heavenly Father who alone is the ultimate sovereign of the universe. This is what heaven meant for black slaves. The idea of heaven provided ways for black people to affirm their humanity when other

people were attempting to define them as non-persons. It enabled blacks to say yes to their right to be free by affirming God's promise to the oppressed of the freedom to be. That was what they meant when they sang about a 'city called heaven.'" He concludes this analysis with the lyrics to "I Am a Poor Pilgrim of Sorrow." Cone, *Spirituals and the Blues*, 91. Lyrics are in the public domain.

[29]In a concert in Tokyo, Japan, in 1967, Joan Baez says she learned "Pilgrim of Sorrow" from a girl at the Sixteenth Street Baptist Church in Birmingham and specifically mentions the four little girls killed in the bombing there. During an intro to the song, she mentions all of the singing done in the movement, and says, "When you can't retaliate against hurt and humiliation, singing is one of the best things to do." A recording of this concert can be found online at www.youtube.com/watch?v=veXOWrN9cOY.

[30]Story told in Branch, *At Canaan's Edge*, 529.

[31]I owe appreciation to Dr. Patrick Smith for sharing this video and his insight with me.

[32]*Autobiography of Martin Luther King, Jr.*, 76-78.

[33]"But If Not," sermon given at Ebenezer Baptist Church, November 5, 1967, accessed July 5, 2018, https://archive.org/details/MlkButIfNot. It's worth noting that King shifted from the biblical example to quoting a song. He could not escape the words of the songs of encouragement that had worked into his heart.

[34]*Autobiography of Martin Luther King, Jr.*, 184.

[35]*Autobiography of Martin Luther King, Jr.*, 185-86.

CONCLUSION: THE WATER IS DEEP, BUT THE BOTTOM IS GOOD

[1]Mother Teresa to Father Neuner, March 6, 1962, in *Come Be My Light: The Private Writings of the "Saint of Calcutta,"* ed. Brian Kolodiejchuk, M.C. (New York: Image, 2007), 230.

[2]Charles Spurgeon, "The Single-Handed Conquest," in *Metropolitan Tabernacle Pulpit*, vol. 44, sermon 2567, accessed August 31, 2017, www.spurgeongems.org/sermon/chs2567.pdf.